OPPOSING
VIEWPOINTS®
SERIES

DISCARDED

Prostitution and
Sex Trafficking

Other Books of Related Interest:

Opposing Viewpoints Series

AIDS

American Values

Pornography

Sex

Sexual Violence

Current Controversies Series

Crime

Sexually Transmitted Diseases

At Issue Series

Sexually Transmitted Diseases

"Congress shall make
no law . . . abridging
the freedom of speech,
or of the press."

First Amendment to the U.S. Constitution

The basic foundation of our democracy is the First Amendment guarantee of freedom of expression. The Opposing Viewpoints Series is dedicated to the concept of this basic freedom and the idea that it is more important to practice it than to enshrine it.

OPPOSING VIEWPOINTS® SERIES

Prostitution and Sex Trafficking

Louise Gerdes, Book Editor

GREENHAVEN PRESS
An imprint of Thomson Gale, a part of The Thomson Corporation

Detroit • New York • San Francisco • New Haven, Conn. • Waterville, Maine • London • Munich

Bonnie Szumski, *Publisher*
Helen Cothran, *Managing Editor*

LIBRARY OF CONGRESS CATALOGING-IN-PUBLICATION DATA

Prostitution and Sex Trafficking / Louise Gerdes, book editor
    p. cm. -- (Opposing viewpoints)
  Includes bibliographical references and index.
    0-7377-3329-2 (lib. : alk. paper) -- 0-7377-3330-6 (pbk. : alk. paper)
  1. Prostitution and sex trafficking. 2. Prostitution and sex trafficking--Social aspects. 3. Prostitution and sex trafficking--United States. I. Gerdes, Louise 1953--. II. Opposing viewpoints series (Unnumbered).
  HQ115.P76 2007
  306.74--dc22

                                     2006041078

Printed in the United States of America
10 9 8 7 6 5 4 3 2 1

Contents

Chapter 3: What Factors Contribute to Prostitution and Sex Trafficking?

Chapter 4: What Policies Should Govern Prostitution?

Why Consider Opposing Viewpoints?

> *"The only way in which a human being can make some approach to knowing the whole of a subject is by hearing what can be said about it by persons of every variety of opinion and studying all modes in which it can be looked at by every character of mind. No wise man ever acquired his wisdom in any mode but this."*
>
> John Stuart Mill

In our media-intensive culture it is not difficult to find differing opinions. Thousands of newspapers and magazines and dozens of radio and television talk shows resound with differing points of view. The difficulty lies in deciding which opinion to agree with and which "experts" seem the most credible. The more inundated we become with differing opinions and claims, the more essential it is to hone critical reading and thinking skills to evaluate these ideas. Opposing Viewpoints books address this problem directly by presenting stimulating debates that can be used to enhance and teach these skills. The varied opinions contained in each book examine many different aspects of a single issue. While examining these conveniently edited opposing views, readers can develop critical thinking skills such as the ability to compare and contrast authors' credibility, facts, argumentation styles, use of persuasive techniques, and other stylistic tools. In short, the Opposing Viewpoints Series is an ideal way to attain the higher-level thinking and reading skills so essential in a culture of diverse and contradictory opinions.

In addition to providing a tool for critical thinking, Opposing Viewpoints books challenge readers to question their own strongly held opinions and assumptions. Most people form their opinions on the basis of upbringing, peer pressure, and personal, cultural, or professional bias. By reading carefully balanced opposing views, readers must directly confront new ideas as well as the opinions of those with whom they disagree. This is not to simplistically argue that everyone who reads opposing views will—or should—change his or her opinion. Instead, the series enhances readers' understanding of their own views by encouraging confrontation with opposing ideas. Careful examination of others' views can lead to the readers' understanding of the logical inconsistencies in their own opinions, perspective on why they hold an opinion, and the consideration of the possibility that their opinion requires further evaluation.

Evaluating Other Opinions

To ensure that this type of examination occurs, Opposing Viewpoints books present all types of opinions. Prominent spokespeople on different sides of each issue as well as well-known professionals from many disciplines challenge the reader. An additional goal of the series is to provide a forum for other, less known, or even unpopular viewpoints. The opinion of an ordinary person who has had to make the decision to cut off life support from a terminally ill relative, for example, may be just as valuable and provide just as much insight as a medical ethicist's professional opinion. The editors have two additional purposes in including these less known views. One, the editors encourage readers to respect others' opinions—even when not enhanced by professional credibility. It is only by reading or listening to and objectively evaluating others' ideas that one can determine whether they are worthy of consideration. Two, the inclusion of such viewpoints encourages the important critical thinking skill of objectively evaluating an author's credentials and bias. This evaluation will illuminate an author's reasons for taking a particular stance on an issue and will aid in readers' evaluation of the author's ideas.

It is our hope that these books will give readers a deeper understanding of the issues debated and an appreciation of the complexity of even seemingly simple issues when good and honest people disagree. This awareness is particularly important in a democratic society such as ours in which people enter into public debate to determine the common good. Those with whom one disagrees should not be regarded as enemies but rather as people whose views deserve careful examination and may shed light on one's own.

Thomas Jefferson once said that "difference of opinion leads to inquiry, and inquiry to truth." Jefferson, a broadly educated man, argued that "if a nation expects to be ignorant and free . . . it expects what never was and never will be." As individuals and as a nation, it is imperative that we consider the opinions of others and examine them with skill and discernment. The Opposing Viewpoints Series is intended to help readers achieve this goal.

David L. Bender and Bruno Leone,
Founders

Introduction

> "Child sex tourism must be stopped. . . .
> To do this, nations must learn from one
> another and work together to draft ef-
> fective legislation that can address all
> issues surrounding child sexual exploi-
> tation."
>
> —Amy Fraley, St. Johns
> Law Review, *Spring 2005.*

In a Dominican Republic bar, a 65-year-old American man points to two prostitutes, ages 12 and 13, and tells United Nations International Children's Educational Fund (UNICEF) researchers, "These girls here, they're always ready. They love sex; it's a natural love of sex. . . . They let you do things here an American girl'd never dream of doing; . . . it's shocking what they'll do just to please you. . . . They'll let you beat them and they get excited. It turns them on." Child sex tourists, those who travel from their own country to another, usually less developed, country to engage in sexual acts with children, often use such rationalizations to justify their behavior—behavior that would be illegal in their native country. Despite worldwide efforts to eliminate child sex tourism, the industry has grown. UNICEF estimates that more than 1 million children are forced into prostitution every year. According to World Vision, a Christian relief organization, "Many of these children are either sold into prostitution to pay off family debts or forcibly recruited on the street to work in brothels, where they are required to have sex with as many as 30 men each day. Some prostituted children are just 5 years old."

Initially, international attention focused on child sex tourism in Thailand and other countries of Southeast Asia. However, the National Center for Missing and Exploited Children

(NCMEC) maintains that "there is no hemisphere, continent, or region unaffected by this trade. As countries develop their economies and tourism industries, sex tourism seems to surface." Few analysts dispute that child sex tourism is a heinous practice that should be eradicated. Activists and policy makers do, however, contest the root causes of child sex tourism and the policies that would best address the problem. Those who attribute child sex tourism to political and cultural conditions that create a supply of child prostitutes advocate policies that urge host nations to enact and enforce laws that oppose prostitution. Such laws, they say, would limit the supply. Those who blame child sex tourism on consumers who create a demand for child prostitutes recommend laws that punish sex tourists, thereby reducing the demand. Such arguments over supply and demand are central to all debates over prostitution.

Analysts who blame the problem of child sex tourism on governments that tolerate prostitution link the growth of tourism in developing nations with a corresponding growth in sex tourism. According to NCMEC, "To many governments around the world, international tourism can be the answer to economic growth and development." However, because of the overall benefits of tourism, NCMEC claims, governments often turn a blind idea to its darker side—sex tourism. Indeed, End Child Prostitution and Trafficking (ECPAT) reports, "The growth of the sex sector is closely tied to economic progress and modernization, and it may be an intentional policy of some countries to promote prostitution as an economic activity." In fact, ECPAT researchers maintain, "Corrupt politicians, police, armed forces and civil servants . . . receive bribes, demand sexual favors and are themselves customers or owners of brothels." Since such conditions provide sex tourists with a supply of child prostitutes, organizations such as ECPAT and NCMEC recommend policies that force host nations to severely punish pimps and brothel owners. Such laws, these analysts reason, will reduce child sex tourism.

Other observers claim that customers—the sex tourists who create the demand for child prostitutes—are responsible for the growth of child sex tourism. Efforts by sex tourists to normalize sex with children in destination countries encourage the practice, they maintain. "[The] racist attitudes of sex tourists cause them to be blind to the harm they cause," argues Kathy J. Steinman in *Hastings Women's Law Journal*. Some sex tourists maintain that the people in the nations they visit are less sexually inhibited and that their culture condones sex with children. Sex tourists to the Dominican Republic, ECPAT researchers maintain, "buy into a highly sexualised form of racism. Without exception, the sex tourists we interviewed described Dominican culture as sexually 'open', 'natural' and 'free.'"

Other sex tourists believe that they are helping the prostituted children they visit. A retired schoolteacher traveling in Latin America told UNICEF researchers that he was "helping [the young girls] financially." Explaining his behavior, he added, "If they don't have sex with me, they may not have enough food. If someone has a problem with me doing this, let UNICEF feed them. I've never paid more than $20 to these young women, and that allows them to eat for a week." Many activists argue that sex tourists must be held accountable for their behavior both at home and in the nations to which they travel. These organizations support laws that harshly punish those who travel to developing nations to have sex with children.

The controversy over the impact of supply and demand on child sex tourism is reflective of the controversy over supply and demand in the broader prostitution and sex trafficking debate. Policy makers must decide whether to focus on the suppliers of sex or its consumers when crafting laws. The authors in this volume explore this and other issues surrounding prostitution and sex trafficking in the following chapters of *Opposing Viewpoints: Prostitution and Sex Trafficking*: Is Prostitution and Sex Trafficking a Serious Problem? How Should Society View Prostitution? What Factors Contribute to Prostitution and Sex Trafficking? and What Policies Should Govern Prostitution and Sex Trafficking?

CHAPTER 1

OPPOSING
VIEWPOINTS®
SERIES

Is Prostitution a Serious Problem?

Chapter Preface

Few analysts dispute that sex trafficking—the purchase, sale, recruitment, harboring, transportation, transfer, or receipt of a person for the purpose of commercial sex—is a serious crime with devastating consequences for its victims. Commentators do, however, dispute the scope of the problem. Some claim that the problem is widespread while others contend it is exaggerated. Since the number of those trafficked will vary depending on how broadly sex trafficking is defined, the definition of sex trafficking has become a hotly contested issue, one of several controversies in the debate over whether prostitution is a serious problem.

Those whose goal is the global abolition of prostitution define all prostitution as a form of slavery. Prostitution, abolitionists argue, is indistinguishable from sex trafficking. Abolitionists therefore include in the number of victims trafficked those who claim to have voluntarily chosen a life of prostitution. According to Wendy Wright of Concerned Women of America, a conservative women's organization that advocates family values, attempts to distinguish coerced from voluntary prostitution inhibit sex trafficking prevention efforts. "If the illegality of an action swings on whether the person was willing or manipulated," Wright claims, "there will be an enticement to create the perception that the victim volunteered." Sex traffickers, she maintains, will therefore coerce victims to lie to authorities using the same techniques they use to ensnare and enslave sex trafficking victims: assaulting and threatening the victim and her family members, inducing drug dependency, confiscating passports and visas, and threatening immigrant victims with incarceration or deportation. Wright also believes that forcing victims to prove that they have been coerced unfairly shifts the burden to sex trafficking victims. "Psychologically and physically traumatized women and girls, as well as males, would be the target of questioning by police and juries," she asserts. "They would have to prove they were beaten, verify how many times they were forced to perform sex, or substantiate that threats were made against them," argues Wright.

Critics of sweeping abolitionist policies contend that a broad definition of sex trafficking does not help prostitutes but instead further threatens their lives and livelihood. "The moral imperative to rescue women from brothels is compelling when young girls are involved or there is clear evidence of duress," claims Susan A. Cohen, writing for the Alan Guttmacher Institute, an organization that supports women's reproductive rights. She adds, "But 'rescuing' adult women from brothels against their will can mean an end to their health care and economic survival. In countries and situations in which basic survival is a daily struggle, the distinction between free agency and oppression may be more a gray area than a bright line." Lisa Katayama, writing for *Mother Jones*, agrees. "Nobody denies that trafficking is an important issue. By some counts, up to 40 million women have been enslaved worldwide," she contends. "Nevertheless," Katayama claims, "the issue is not always as simple as it appears, and all too often crackdowns on trafficking end up cracking down on—and hurting—women who are simply trying to make a living in the sex industry, insisting on the right to ply their trade." Human rights advocates maintain that the failure to distinguish between coerced and voluntary prostitution have led to one-dimensional laws such as the Trafficking Victims Protection Act, which "are too simplistic, and often do as much harm as good."

Activists and policy makers continue to debate whether sex trafficking should be distinguished from voluntary prostitution. The authors in the following chapter debate this and other issues concerning the nature and scope of prostitution and sex trafficking in order to determine which policies will best serve women and children worldwide.

> "The activities of the commercial sex in-
> dustry in the United States continue to
> create an enormous demand for victims
> of domestic and international sex
> trafficking."

Sex Trafficking Threatens the United States

Jennifer Goodson

Sex trafficking victims from around the world are held captive in residential neighborhoods across the United States, maintains Jennifer Goodson in the following viewpoint. Many victims are poor, sexually abused children and young adults who are easily seduced by promises of a better life, Goodson asserts. Once recruited or smuggled into the United States, victims are psychologically and physically abused and forced to work as prostitutes, she claims. Goodson, an anti-trafficking activist, is director of international programs for Shared Hope International.

As you read, consider the following questions:

1. In Goodson's opinion, how is trafficking in persons defined?
2. According to the author, how do some pimps enforce their "code of conduct"?

Jennifer Goodson, "Exploiting Body and Soul: Sex Trafficking Is Big Business Around the World—and the Root of That Business Is Closer to Home than You Might Think," *Sojourners*, vol. 34, September-October 2005, p. 20. Copyright © 2005 Sojourners. Reproduced with permission from Sojourners. www.sojo.net.

3. What common thread runs between the commercial sex industry and trafficking, in the author's opinion?

"Susannah" [whose name has been changed to protect her identity] was raped by her stepfather when she was 11 years old. The exploitation at home spurred her to run away. On the streets, she was recruited by a gang in Cape Town, South Africa, managed by Nigerian organized-crime syndicates. For girls, initiation into the gang includes being raped and prostituted by the boys in the gang. In the gang lair, Susannah was introduced to drugs and repeatedly raped. By the time Susannah turned 12, she had already been betrayed by her family, raped at home and on the street, and was addicted to drugs.

I first met Susannah at a conference on resource programs for exploited women and children hosted by Shared Hope International. This beautiful 18-year-old woman from South Africa had been out of the gang less than a year before my meeting with her. In the midst of our meetings she shocked us with her bold statement: "I am a person!" It was a magnificent moment celebrating the recognition of her dignity.

Susannah told us about being "independent" during her life of prostitution, although she was managed by a pimp, and her "clients" from Nigeria, the United States, and Australia introduced her to drugs and facilitated her habit. A girlfriend in a treatment program introduced her to Satanism. Susannah told us about rituals that included getting tattoos while renouncing the person of Jesus. When I first met her she had 13 tattoos—one, on her stomach, was of an upside-down cross.

Restoring Hope

After six years of exploitation by both men and women, Susannah had no idea that Jacobus and Erica Nomdoe were building a community to rescue and restore young women like her. The Nomdoes are a South African couple who care for troubled youth in Cape Town gangs. Working with their church and Teen Challenge International, the Nomdoes established a deferral system with the juvenile courts and a residential and vocational training center for teen boys. When they met Susannah and five other girls in a similar situation, they opened the doors of their own home and took them in. In the Nomdoes' home, the girls found safety and hope.

I met the Nomdoes while traveling in South Africa in 2004 with former U.S. member of Congress Linda Smith—who founded Shared Hope International in 1998—to plan an international summit on sex trafficking. The Nomdoes and their community made themselves available to very troubled youth, including those who were trafficked within South Africa. Their stories, although told by workers on the verge of burnout, were filled with hope. We were eager to do something to help. Thanks to generous donors we returned six months later to celebrate the dedication of the "Home of Hope," which now cares for young girls and women in Cape Town.

Through the Nomdoes I learned that human dignity can not be reduced to a language of self-actualization, discovery, and esteem. Human dignity is rooted in our relationship to our Creator. Oppression is not only the marring and exploitation of the person but the suppression of the divine image intended to be reflected in that person.

Susannah's story is one of millions that can be told about youth who are betrayed by their families, left vulnerable to criminal networks, and exploited in excruciating ways. In the categories we create for injustice, we could name Susannah as a victim of domestic violence, gang rape, drug abuse, and more. But would we look at this story and call it trafficking?

Defining Trafficking

"Trafficking in persons" is primarily understood as the movement of persons across international boundaries for a variety of forms of exploitation. The crime of trafficking, of course, is not essentially about the movement of the person but about the exploitation. Trafficking is the denial of freedom.

Trafficking exists in many forms, each deserving very aggressive and specific initiatives to combat it. If people of faith are to understand the nature of trafficking that is done to prostitute others and other forms of sexual exploitation, they must address not only specific acts but also the broad range of issues that allow this form of exploitation to exist.

Trafficking is a global issue that takes root in almost every culture. In 2004, the U.S. State Department estimated that up to 18,500 men, women, and children are trafficked into the United States every year, some for forced labor and others for sexual exploitation. Estimates of the number of women and children who are trafficked across international borders each year range from 800,000 to 4 million. These numbers don't take into account those moved from rural areas to urban centers within their own countries. For example, these numbers don't include women and youth who are moved from the Hill Tribes of Northern Thailand to Bangkok or who are recruited from rural Appalachia and moved to Baltimore.

An American Problem

In the United States, victims of international sex trafficking come primarily from South and Southeast Asia, Eastern Europe, Latin America, and Africa. They are held captive in residential and commercial sex industry businesses throughout the United States. More than 170 cases of trafficking have been prosecuted by the Department of Justice and the U.S. Attorney's office since the Trafficking Victims Protection Act was passed in 2000; 131 of those cases involved sex trafficking. Those offices have secured 120 convictions in trafficking; 99 of those 120 defendants were convicted of sex trafficking.

In April 2005, the Justice Department and the U.S. Attorney's office for the Eastern District of New York had a major victory when three defendants pled guilty to all 27

The United States Is a Major Importer of Sex Slaves

The United States has become a major importer of sex slaves. [In 2003], the C.I.A. estimated that between 18,000 and 20,000 people are trafficked annually into the United States. The government has not studied how many of these are victims of sex traffickers, but Kevin Bales, president of Free the Slaves, America's largest anti-slavery organization, says that the number is at least 10,000 a year. John Miller, the State Department's director of the Office to Monitor and Combat Trafficking in Persons, conceded: "That figure could be low. What we know is that the number is huge." Bales estimates that there are 30,000 to 50,000 sex slaves in captivity in the United States at any given time. Laura Lederer, a senior State Department adviser on trafficking, told me, "We're not finding victims in the United States because we're not looking for them."

Peter Landesman, New York Times Magazine, *January 25, 2004.*

counts of an indictment charging them with forcing young Mexican women to engage in commercial sex acts. The prostitution occurred in brothels throughout the New York City metropolitan area over a 14-year period. The defendants admitted to recruiting numerous young, uneducated Mexican women from impoverished backgrounds, smuggling them into the United States, and forcing them into prostitution. They described using physical force on the women, which led to serious injuries, and forcing the women to "service" several men a day.

Victims of domestic sex trafficking (those trafficked within the borders of the United States) are not well documented, but they are recruited from both rural and urban areas into the commercial sex industry. New Horizons Ministries in Seattle runs an outreach program working with street youth, including those involved in prostitution. Between June 2004 and June 2005, outreach workers recorded 772 interactions with women below the age of 23.

One girl they work with, Jasmine, was recruited by a man at a bus stop when she was 13 years old. She grew up in an impoverished family and was sexually abused at home. She was a prime target for a pimp who promised to provide her with beautiful clothes, love, and a promising future. Instead she got cycles of violence and exploitation from which she couldn't escape. From the time Jasmine was 14 until she was 17, her pimp had her on a prostitution circuit that moved between Las Vegas, San Diego, Portland, and Seattle.

Atlanta is also a hub for sex trafficking. In August 2004, two men were convicted and sentenced for conspiring to participate in a juvenile prostitution ring—enticing juveniles into prostitution and into involuntary servitude. The girls, in this case, were all from the United States; some as young as 12. The pimps' known activity occurred between 1997 and 2001 when they were arrested. The trial revealed the elaborate nature of the pimping networks, culture, and methods for enslaving the juveniles as prostitutes. The CEOs of this ring had created their own training video titled Pimps Up, Ho's Down that outlined the "code of conduct" for pimps and prostitutes. To enforce their code, the pimps often beat the youth with belts, baseball bats, or "pimp sticks" (two coat hangers wrapped together). The pimps also forced them to lay naked on the floor and have sex with another prostitute while others watched. One of the men was sentenced to a total of 30 years in prison.

A Common Thread

The activities of the commercial sex industry in the United States continue to create an enormous demand for victims of domestic and international sex trafficking. The common thread between the commercial sex industry and trafficking? Servitude and exploitation.

People of faith are already active in neighborhoods and initiatives where they find victims of international and domestic sex trafficking. Urban renewal projects, addiction recovery facilities, immigrant social services, domestic violence shelters, juvenile justice programs, and youth ministries are places where one might encounter a victim of trafficking—if you know what to look for.

We are all called to honor and summon out the true human dignity of the people in our midst, whether in boardrooms or on the streets—especially when, like Susannah before her escape from gang life and thousands of others still trapped in the economy of human slavery, they don't perceive it in themselves.

| *"The uptick [of sex trafficking] isn't that significant in a nation of almost 300 million."*

The Problem of Sex Trafficking in the United States Is Overstated

Jack Shafer

In the following viewpoint Jack Shafer argues that the sex trafficking epidemic in the United States has been exaggerated. Although sex trafficking is a horrific problem, overzealous journalists and activists overstate the number of victims in the United States and contradict statistics reported by the U.S. State Department, he asserts. Moreover, trafficking statistics do not distinguish between those trafficked as sex slaves from those trafficked for other purposes, Shafer maintains, so the number of those trafficked for sex remains unknown. Shafer is an editor for Slate, *an online magazine of news and commentary.*

As you read, consider the following questions:

1. How does the United States Code define trafficking?
2. How does Shafer describe the estimates of sex victims trafficked provided by Kevin Bales and John R. Miller?
3. What is a T-1 visa, according to Shafer?

Jack Shafer, "Sex Slaves, Revisited," *Slate.com,* June 7, 2005. Copyright © 2006 Washington Newsweek Interactive Co. LLC. Distributed by United Feature Syndicate, Inc.

"Left unchallenged, even the wildest guesses take on the certitude of fact," reporter Christopher S. Wren wrote in 1997. Wren's subject was the size and scope of the drug problem, but he could have been writing about the number of sex slaves working in American brothels, a subject about which I burned many pixels in this space [in February 2004].

What provoked me was Peter Landesman's cover story in the Jan. 25, 2004, *New York Times Magazine*, "The Girls Next Door." In language that glowed both purple and yellow, Landesman conjured a vision of an international "sex-trafficking epidemic" and the nightmare of tens of thousands of women and girls smuggled annually into the United States, held prisoner, and forced to service johns for the benefit of their pimps.

Uncertain Figures

To be sure, sex slavery in the United States is real and horrific, but the body count remains anybody's guess, and that includes the U.S. government. Since releasing its first "Trafficking in Persons Report" in 2001, the State Department's estimate of the total number "trafficked" annually across international borders has stayed pretty constant, varying between 600,000 and 900,000. (The U.S. Code defines trafficking in part as the use of force or coercion—violent or psychological—to exploit a person for commercial sex or the recruitment, transportation, or provision of a person for any form of involuntary servitude, debt bondage, or slavery.) In 2001, the State Department estimated that between 45,000 and 50,000 people were annually trafficked to the U.S. The 2002 report was silent on the total trafficked but confidently cited a 1997 estimate stating that 50,000 women and children were trafficked here annually "for sexual exploitation." In 2003, the State Department report estimated that 18,000 to 20,000 individuals were trafficked here for forced labor *and* sexual exploitation. The June 2004 report, published after Landesman's ar-

Blinded by an Agenda

The activists against sexual slavery ... are engaged in an admirable cause. But, like many advocates, they can be blinded by their agenda. [Laura] Lederer, for instance, tells [*New York Times* reporter Peter] Landesman that "We're not finding victims [of sexual slavery] in the United States because we're not looking for them"—a statement that has some truth in it, but may also be a convenient way to explain the lack of evidence.

Cathy Young, Boston Globe, *February 9, 2004.*

ticle appeared, set the total trafficked annually at between 14,500 and 17,500.

Landesman complained in one paragraph of his piece about how little work had been done to quantify the number of sex victims trafficked into the U.S. and then in the next paragraph quoted a pulled-out-of-thin-air estimate by Kevin Bales, president of the advocacy group Free the Slaves, that at least 10,000 new sex slaves joined the count each year. Landesman also quoted the similarly manufactured estimate of State Department official John R. Miller, who said Bales' figure "could be low. What we know is that the number is huge." Bales further speculated that between 30,000 and 50,000 sex slaves were being held captive on these shores at any time.

Conflicting Reports

None of these conjectures conform with the 2005 State Department report on trafficking, released [in May 2005]. The report stays the course of other recent estimates, stating that between 600,000 and 800,000 are trafficked across borders each year. It doesn't venture a total U.S. trafficked number, but a June [3, 2005] news story by the Voice of America attributes a figure of 15,000 to Miller. The *New York Times* also reports the 15,000 number. So much for the "epidemic" Landesman posited in his piece.

How many of the people in this new trafficking estimate are sex slaves remains a mystery. According to the report, total U.S. Department of Justice investigations, prosecutions, and convictions of trafficking cases are up in the last four fiscal years (2001–2004) compared to the previous four years. But because the statistics don't break out sex-trafficking cases from total trafficking cases, they're not very useful. In any event, the uptick isn't that significant in a nation of almost 300 million: 118 trafficking defendants were convicted in the last four years versus 59 in the previous four-year period.

Because sexual slavery is the most depraved form of involuntary servitude, one would expect that if sex slaves existed in the numbers Landesman, Bales, and Miller would have us believe, more of them would have applied for the heavily publicized "T-1 visa." Of course it takes enormous courage and a view of daylight for a sex slave to break away even temporarily from a captor and apply for this visa, which allows qualified non-immigrant victims of trafficking to live in the U.S. for three years and apply for permanent residency. Yet in fiscal year 2004, only 520 T-visa applications were received, and that includes all T-1s as well as the lesser visas for the spouses (T-2), children (T-3), and parents (T-4) of the trafficked, according to the State Department's 2005 report. Of those applications, 136 were granted, 292 denied, and 92 are pending. The 2004 report recorded only 374 requests for T visas. Can there be tens of thousands of sex slaves in the country, growing by tens of thousands each year, and only a handful applying for help?

None of this is to suggest that sex slaves don't exist. They do, as a casual Nexis search will confirm. But 16 months after the publication of "The Girls Next Door," Landesman's wild guesses and shocking narrative have still not acquired a scintilla of certitude.

> "More than 700,000 of those trafficked
> are women and children sold into pros-
> titution or forced labour. ... Many are
> East European women and girls from
> impoverished rural areas."

Eastern European Sex Slavery Is a Serious Problem

Irena Maryniak

Sex traffickers promise Eastern European women legitimate jobs in the West and Middle East, argues Irena Maryniak in the following viewpoint, but once these women reach their destination, traffickers sell them into sexual slavery. Since the fall of communism, Eastern European women are particularly vulnerable because they have few economic opportunities under the new regimes and are easily lured away from home by an idealized vision of life in the West, she asserts. Maryniak is Eastern Europe editor of Index on Censorship.

As you read, consider the following questions:

1. In Maryniak's opinion, how are victims of sex trafficking recruited?

2. In the author's view, how has the feminization of poverty created excellent conditions for trafficking?

3. According to the author, why is there no effective escape for victims of trafficking?

Irena Maryniak, "The New Slave Trade," *Index on Censorship,* vol. 32, April 2003. Reproduced by permission of the publisher, www.indexonline.org.

Human trafficking is one of the most lucrative businesses in the world. UN[United Nations] estimates suggest that the 4 million people moved across international borders by traffickers each year generate profits of up to US$7 billion, subsequently laundered and fed into other activities including drugs and arms smuggling.

More than 700,000 of those trafficked are women and children sold into prostitution or forced labour. Sex slaves working in Europe account for about two-thirds of this figure. Many are East European women and girls from impoverished rural areas, who had hoped to flee unemployment, family restrictions and conflict at home for a better life abroad. Victims are recruited by boyfriends, family members and trusted female friends, or through seemingly reputable employment, travel or marriage agencies. Some are as young as 13. They may be offered jobs in fashion, tourism, housekeeping, catering or entertainment in Western Europe, with promises of travel documents, transport, comfortable accommodation, even education. Occasionally they are kidnapped. About 20 per cent may be aware of the possibility of becoming involved in sex-related work but none expects to be enslaved.

Women Bear the Burden

The collapse of the Berlin Wall and simpler exit procedures have increased freedom of movement in Eastern Europe, but factors such as inadequate education, idealised notions of life in the West, legislation favourable to the commercial sex industry in many countries, and particularly the feminisation of poverty have created excellent conditions for trafficking. In parts of Russia women represent 70–95 per cent of the unemployed. Throughout the former communist bloc public childcare centres have been closed, social security structures dismantled, pensions reduced. This has left women carrying the burden of care and breadwinning, with less access than ever to the labour sector. Opportunities for careers or political participation have been blunted; women are poorly paid, the first to be dismissed, and may have to offer sex to their bosses to stay in a job. 'Central Eastern Europe is comparable to Latin America or the Philippines in terms of women's desperation,' says Gyorgyi Toth, director of NANE, a Hungarian NGO[non-governmental organization] that campaigns against domestic violence.

At home, and in the informal sector of charring [house-keeping] and sexual services to which so many women are relegated, physical abuse is widely accepted. For women from Ukraine, Russia, Moldova, Romania, Belarus or Bulgaria there seems to be little to lose and everything to gain in risking a job abroad or simply away from family pressures. Their notional destination may be a Western European country or a big city closer to home, but once in the hands of the trafficking network, the victims lose any power to decide for themselves. They are coerced by violence, rape, food deprivation and drugs: the procedure is called 'seasoning'. They are forced to give up passports and money, and stay locked in their accommodation until allowed out by their pimps to work as prostitutes. They may find themselves shunted via Albania or former Yugoslavia to almost any country in Western or Northern Europe, Turkey, Israel, the US or the United Arab Emirates. During the course of a journey from Moldova to Kosovo, for example, a woman may be bought and sold up to six times. In the country of destination designated for her by the traffickers, she will be obliged to repay 'debts' consisting of the cost of her documents and transport, or her purchase price, which can range from US$700 to US$2,500. She will have no protection from STDs or AIDS, and will receive medical care on an emergency basis only, especially if her symptoms threaten to affect her 'performance'.

A Brutal Business

Sex trafficking is denied and trivialised by the authorities and media in many regions, and the women see police not as a potential source of help but of harassment. Prosecution of offenders and assistance to victims are not high priorities, and corruption is rife. The international community has offered few preventive initiatives and little assistance to victims, although some EU [European Union] funding has gone to East European NGOs and the International Organisation for Migration has run awareness campaigns in a number of countries. The Special Trafficking Operation Programme (STOP), launched in 2001 by the UN in Bosnia, led to revelations about the involvement of the International Police Task Force and the Stabilisation Force (SFOR) in sex trafficking, and to an increase in prosecutions. But it also helped to push the business underground. Police raids simply encourage gangs to change their routes and relocate.

For the victims there is no effective escape. One way to get out is to recruit others, but women who do find their way home are often dragged back into the prostitution network by blackmail and threats against themselves and their families. It is a brutal fact that as public awareness rises the trafficking business becomes ever more violent and dangerous.

The Story of 'Marinella', Romanian

Back home I had no income. My grandmother had her pension, my mother got child benefits for three children, and the alimony. My brother's best friend was an exchange dealer, he'd been visiting our house for years. He'd eaten with us, he'd sat with my father and brother at the same table.

His name is Ion. I don't know his other name, in our town they all call him Manet ('handle'). I said to him, 'Manet, if you're taking me away to make a whore of me, don't do it, brother. Don't take me away from my child.' And he said, 'If I didn't know your family and your brother, maybe I'd do it, but as it is, I won't.' So I went, telling myself that in a month I'd be sending money to my mother.

My brother's girlfriend went too. He said he was taking us to Italy, and that once we were there he'd take me to a pizzeria to do the dishes, and her to a bar (because she could speak Italian) to work as a sort of bartender. I had a passport, but my brother's girlfriend didn't and he took us over to Serbia by boat. I asked why weren't we going through customs, I was afraid of water, I argued with him for at least an hour. Eventually they talked me into doing it and he said I'd cross the next border with the passport. So I crossed over into Macedonia with my passport and the others went through a forest.

There were three girls and four boys—two of them said they also wanted to get to Italy—and we all left for Skopje. We stayed in an apartment, the boys went off, and we moved to another place where there were 40 girls staying. I thought they were all living there.

The girls all wanted to get to Italy to work as photo models, as cooks or in hotels. They had been promised large sums of money. When I heard from the Russian and Moldovan girls that we were going to be sold and become prostitutes, I couldn't believe my ears. I tried to kill myself. For one and a half months I couldn't call home. I have a little girl . . . no, no . . . I can't find the words, I didn't think I'd ever get home.

A week later, some guys came over and looked at us, but we still didn't know we were being sold. A few days later somebody took me and two other girls to an Albanian's house in Macedonia, near the border with Albania.

Sold into Slavery

There were 200 girls living in the villa. We were held there until we could be sold for a higher price. The girls were Russian, Romanian; many of them had run away, been captured and returned by police in Bulgaria, and sold back.

Four of us would share a hamburger, there was a packet of cigarettes for eight girls. That was all the food we had in a day. He beat us. We'd ask for water, and got 20 litres in plastic

Sex Slavery in the United Kingdom

Paul Holmes, a former inspector in the [London Metropolitan Police], for six years operational head of the Vice Unit at Charing Cross . . . works as a consultant for the [International Organisation for Migration]. . . . Holmes has said many times that the influx of women from Eastern Europe into the [United Kingdom] vice trade is out of control. 'Over 90 per cent of the women who come back have been victims of deception, usually with false job promises, and have been forced into sexual slavery,' he says. 'They're all damaged, many badly. It's a huge problem here.'

John Gibb, Observer, February 23, 2003.

bottles. That had to be enough for the day. We had to wash, we couldn't stay like that, and if we wanted to use the lavatory, it was only allowed at certain times. We were starved.

None of the girls had passports, but I was left with my identity card. They even took our clothes away. In Albania I was beaten. Once I ate nothing for four days. Before I was taken away, I hadn't gone out for a week. My eyebrow arch was broken, he'd hit me with a pistol on the head, and said he'd shoot me. The Albanian's mistress was a Moldovan, she could speak Romanian and she was our boss. And she hit us whenever there was something she didn't like. I was afraid. Maybe I wouldn't have given in, but then I saw they meant what they said. They killed a girl in front of me and buried her behind the house. She was only 17.

The owner's mistress was distantly related to her. The girl had shouted at her and said she'd tell the owner's wife about their relationship. So the mistress went and complained to the owner, who was drunk. He came and trampled her, he held on to the wall and kept jumping on her, and then he lifted her up and threw her against the wall. I think that was when everything broke inside her because the wall was all splashed with blood. She was lying there moaning, with blood gushing from her eyes, her ears, everywhere, her mouth, her nose, and then he took out his pistol and shot her dead and dragged her outside. He ordered us to clean the floor, the wall was going to be whitewashed later. Five or six days after that, we were sold.

For three days I wasn't able to raise a cigarette to my mouth, I was trembling all over, I was having nightmares about her, I can see it in my mind right now. He wasn't a human being.

Looking for Help

In all the bars where I worked, the girls were beaten and starved. If they wouldn't dance or go with a customer, they got nothing to eat. In Gostivar there was a cop from the airport . . . I asked him to help me, I gave him my address, I gave him everything, and he went to the owner and told him I wanted to escape and report him to the police . . . I didn't trust anyone any more. The policemen from Gostivar came—in uniform and in plain clothes—they had girlfriends, *falice* they called them. When a more serious inspection was to take place, they'd tell the owner and he'd hide us . . . Important men came from Skopje—the police used to announce their arrival . . . senators . . . They knew about our situation and our life there, but they didn't care.

A nephew of his took me away in secret and said he'd take me home. He said he loved me, but he sold me . . . me and another girl. He sold her too, in Albania, but to a different person. Our former owner wanted to sell us for a very high price and nobody would buy us. This guy said we had a hard life, we were suffering, he'd take us home.....

I fell ill, otherwise he wouldn't have let me go. There was snow, I ran out and stood barefoot in the snow, in my dress, and fell seriously ill, and needed medical treatment. I had a haemorrhage, they took me to hospital and they couldn't stop it unless I stayed in. The owner didn't want to leave me there. But he knew a police raid was due that night and the girls were to be rounded up. So he gave us up—me and two other girls.

| "*The sad and perhaps unpalatable fact is that most Eastern European women working abroad as prostitutes do so out of choice.*"

The Problem of Eastern European Sex Slavery Is Exaggerated

Phelim McAleer

In the following viewpoint Phelim McAleer maintains that most Eastern European women who travel west to become prostitutes do so by choice. The sensational stories of international sex trafficking rings luring naive, Eastern European girls into sexual slavery are unfounded, he argues. British police officers working in Romania claim that most of the girls going west are seasoned prostitutes lured by the money that they will make, asserts McAleer. He claims that anti-trafficking activists use exaggerated sex-slavery stories to get international media coverage of their cause. McAleer is Romanian correspondent for the Financial Times, *a British newsmagazine.*

As you read, consider the following questions:

1. According to McAleer, what is suspiciously similar about sex-slave stories?

2. In the author's view, why are Romanian, Moldovan, and Ukranian prostitutes tempted to work in the West?

3. Why do accounts of widespread cruelty by brothel owners not stand up to scrutiny, in the author's opinion?

The reports of Eastern European women being forced into prostitution in the West are as numerous as they are horrific. They have worried the government so much that the Home Office [the British justice and immigration department] has plans for a new scheme to provide 'safe-houses' for the victims of sex trafficking. But for many who work with these 'sex slaves' the women's accounts are just that—stories. It is seldom reported, but widely known, that most women volunteer for the trip westward because of the money they can make.

The sex-slave stories are suspiciously similar. The women are usually from some deprived backwater. They have naively answered advertisements for jobs as waitresses or nannies in the West. However, when they arrived to start their new life, their documents were confiscated, they were beaten and raped into submission, and forced to become prostitutes. They then claimed to have been kept as sex slaves, sometimes chained to beds, terrified and servicing as many customers as the brothel owner demanded.

According to the International Office of Migration [IOM] which rescues and shelters these women, there are an estimated 400,000 enduring this existence. But as anyone who works closely with the prostitutes and who isn't infected with victimitis knows, the IOM version of events is nonsense.

Making a Choice

Take Assistant Chief Constable Andy Felton, a British police officer who has been working in Romania [since 2000]. Most of his time has been spent on Project Reflex, a unique Romanian/British venture to stem illegal immigration into the

UK. As part of the initiative, Felton has interrogated those deported from the UK. 'Some are tricked into becoming prostitutes, but the overwhelming majority of girls going to the West understand before they leave that they will be working in prostitution,' says Felton.

He has found that far from being gullible peasant girls, as portrayed by the IOM, most were seasoned prostitutes before they left. For brothel owners 'experience is essential'; it makes poor business sense to trick unsuspecting girls into the trade. Those without experience but who still want to go are tried out in the nearest big city to avoid making a dud investment.

So the sad and perhaps unpalatable fact is that most Eastern European women working abroad as prostitutes do so out of choice. This choice may be dictated by appalling poverty and lack of opportunity in their home countries but it is, nonetheless, a choice.

The minimum salary in Romania is $50 a month—even less in Moldova and Ukraine. It is not surprising that many women become sex workers, if only to support their families. But if the punters [customers] are all living on tiny wages, the amount left over for prostitutes will also be small. No wonder the temptation to do the same work in the West for $100 a client proves just too tempting.

The Sex-Slave Myth

In the sex-slave myth, the recruiters scour Eastern Europe with smooth talk and big promises. These latter-day big bad wolves lure women with offers of jobs and a bright future. A frightening scenario, indeed. It just isn't true. 'There is no huge international prostitute recruiting team travelling around Central and Eastern Europe. There is no fleet of Mercs with blacked-out windows and a madam in the back luring women abroad,' says Felton.

His investigations have found that almost all the women's westward journeys were arranged by someone they know.

The Retelling of an Old Myth

The repetition of core elements of the 'white slavery' myth in accounts of 'trafficking in women': innocence deceived, youthful virginity despoiled, the motifs of disease and death, the depraved black/Jewish/foreign trafficker, point in the direction of a new telling of an old myth. 'Trafficking in women' is the re-telling of the myth of 'white slavery' in a modern form, a new 'moral panic' arising in the context of 'boundary crises' involving fears of loss of community identity. . . . All over the world, communities are caught up in identity crises in the face of displacement, mass migration and globalisation. The myth of 'trafficking in women' is one manifestation of attempts to re-establish community identity, in which race, sexuality and women's autonomy are used as markers and metaphors of crucial boundaries. Thus, while incidents reported in accounts of 'trafficking' may be 'true', they may be at the same time mythical, to the extent that the events are (re)constructed in such a way as to conform to the framework established by the myth.

Jo Doezema, Gender Issues, *Winter 2000.*

'This tends to be a family member, or a local person, or someone who has herself been a prostitute in the West.'

Then there are the traffickers/brothel owners: a particularly well-organised bunch—normally the Albanian mafia—we are told. Again, nice story, nice villain, but just not true. 'It's more a case of, I know someone with a bus in Timisoara and somebody else knows somebody in Italy who will meet them. It is a loose alliance of contacts. There is no huge criminal structure with a mafia godfather running it,' says Felton.

He wishes it were that simple. 'One of the problems tackling these networks is that they are so loose they can easily fall apart,' he says.

Accounts of widespread cruelty by brothel owners are easy to believe, but do not stand up to scrutiny. The owners are in a business that thrives on the customer who visits regularly and very often has a 'relationship' with his favourite girl. No doubt a small number of men get a kick out of seeing women chained to beds or battered and bruised, but for most it would be a turn-off. That is not to say there are not bad and crooked brothel owners. But the women come West voluntarily, and very quickly learn through word of mouth which establishments to avoid.

Despite seldom being reported, Felton's findings are not news to his Romanian counterparts. Major Marin Banica used to be Romania's most senior police officer investigating 'women trafficking'. 'Very few go abroad without knowing exactly why they are going,' he says.

A Sensational Story

However, the Eastern European prostitute as victim is a powerful image, and ever more influential NGOs are reluctant to let the truth get in the way of their story. Take the case of the Cambodia Seven. In 2001, seven Romanian 'sex slaves' were found in Cambodia. Their rescuers, who included the IOM, reported how they had been offered jobs as dancers but were then forced into prostitution. Their plight received international media coverage and was mentioned by Brunson McKinney, the IOM director, at an anti-trafficking conference in Bucharest. He said it was an indication of the growing problem.

Yet, according to Banica, the full story of the Cambodia Seven was not told. Before the Romanian authorities could reach Cambodia to organise bringing the women home, one managed to slip away from her rescuers. Banica does not know where she ended up, but believes she returned to prostitution. Legitimate job opportunities for Romanian women in Cambodia are limited.

Banica does know what happened to the six who returned. 'Within weeks three of the women had gone to work in Albania—again as prostitutes,' he says.

The sex-slave myth also portrays Eastern European women as idiots. Banica asks how hundreds of thousands of women from the same pockets of the country could have been repeatedly tricked. For this to be true, it also means no duped woman has ever come home and, if they have, they have never talked to family and friends about their experiences.

To accept the sex-slave myth, one must also accept that none of the women or their families or friends has ever read a newspaper or watched Romanian television, where the story is given widespread and often sensational coverage. Or maybe they do and that is exacerbating the problem.

A recent Romanian television public-awareness campaign shows faceless men recruiting naive women while salivating over the massive sums of money to be made. The emphasis on the huge amounts of cash available could be all the encouragement that some women need.

| *"There are societal costs of child prostitution, including adverse health effects."*

Child Prostitution Is a Global Health Problem

Brian M. Willis and Barry S. Levy

In the following viewpoint Brian M. Willis of the Centers for Disease Control, and Barry S. Levy, professor of Community Health at Tufts University School of Medicine, contend that child prostitution is a $5 billion industry that poses a serious health threat to children worldwide. Child prostitutes are more likely to become infected with sexually transmitted and other infectious diseases, including HIV, hepatitis, and tuberculosis, the authors assert. Child prostitutes also risk rape and physical abuse and suffer from debilitating mental illness and substance abuse, they claim. Without access to contraception, the authors maintain, many child prostitutes become pregnant, and the babies that survive suffer from similar health problems.

As you read, consider the following questions:

1. What factors do Willis and Levy contend contribute to child prostitution?

2. How does UNICEF characterize child prostitution?

Brian M. Willis and Barry S. Levy, "Child Prostitution: Global Health Burden, Research Needs, and Interventions," *Lancet,* vol. 359, April 20, 2002, pages 1417-1421. Copyright © 2002. Reproduced with permission from Elsevier.

3. What is needed to assess the magnitude of child prostitution, in the authors' opinion?

Child prostitution involves offering the sexual services of a child or inducing a child to perform sexual acts for any form of compensation, financial or otherwise. For the purposes of this article, a child is anyone younger than 18 years, as defined by the UN [United Nations] Convention on the Rights of the Child. Child prostitution differs from child sexual abuse, such as incest or molestation, because it involves commercial exploitation. However, it is similar to child sexual abuse in that children cannot consent to being prostituted because, in addition to child prostitution being illegal and a violation of human rights conventions, children do not have the requisite capacity to make such decisions.

Both girls and boys, some as young as 10 years, are prostituted. Most of these children are exploited by local men, although some are also prostituted by paedophiles and foreign tourists. Some of these children may have five to ten clients per day. The number of prostituted children . . . is thought to be increasing and could be as high as 10 million. Although these children are found in many settings, including on the street or in brothels, hotels, and bars, locating them can be difficult because they are often hidden and frequently moved. Involvement of organised crime creates additional barriers to locating prostituted children.

Contributing Factors

Social, cultural, and economic factors contribute to child prostitution through gender bias, discrimination, poor education, and poverty. For example, in some communities, prostitution is widely accepted, laws against child prostitution are not enforced, or both. In other communities, male clients believe that children are less likely to pass on HIV infection and sexually transmitted diseases (STDs). Children of sex workers are at risk of being prostituted. Homeless, runaway, or abandoned children are frequently pushed into prostitution and actively recruited by pimps and traffickers. Sometimes girls are enticed or kidnapped and then forced into prostitution. In some areas of developing countries, international sex tourism (travel solely for the purpose of having sex) is a significant cause of child prostitution. Finally, in rare cases, families give their children to religious or tribal elders as atonement for adult wrongdoings.

Specific causes of child prostitution might differ between countries and communities. For example, in parts of Nigeria, children fleeing abuse at home are pushed into prostitution, whereas child prostitution in Nepal is attributed to poverty. In the USA, child prostitution is linked with childhood sexual abuse. In some countries, such as Thailand, specific factors contributing to child prostitution differ between regions and often depend on ethnic origin such as being from Bangkok or northern tribal communities.

Poverty and the profitability of prostitution are the main factors that sustain this industry. The sex industry worldwide generates an estimated US$20 billion or more yearly, of which $5 billion is attributed to child prostitution. Prostituted children are often responsible for providing financial support (income remittances) to their families. Strategies to remove children from prostitution must address this issue, lest the lost income simply results in other children being pushed into sex work. Finally, there are societal costs of child prostitution, including adverse health effects and restriction of education.

Human Rights Issues

Child prostitution is a gross violation of children's rights and dignity. UNICEF characterises it as "one of the gravest infringements of rights that children can endure." In Asia, an estimated 1 million children in the sex trade are held in conditions that are indistinguishable from slavery.

Children have a right to be protected from prostitution under the UN Convention on the Rights of the Child. The convention was adopted as an international human rights treaty in 1989, and has been ratified by all countries except the USA and Somalia. Governments are obliged to protect children from prostitution under Article 34 of the convention. Under Article 39, governments must take all appropriate measures to promote the recovery and social reintegration of children who have been exploited. In 2000, the UN adopted an optional protocol to the convention that extends the measures governments must take to protect children from prostitution. Child prostitution has also been described as one of the worst forms of child labour. However, since child prostitution is prohibited under the convention it should not be thought of as a form of labour.

Morbidity and Mortality

Although most reports on child prostitution acknowledge that it results in many serious health problems, there are very few reliable morbidity and mortality data. . . .

We used the few specific health data on prostituted children and data from studies in sex workers and adolescents to estimate the global morbidity and mortality associated with child prostitution. . . .

Sexually Transmitted Diseases

Prostituted children are at high risk of many infectious diseases and their sequelae. In many locations, prostituted children are at high risk of infection with HIV. For example, in a study by the Economic and Social Commission for Asia and the Pacific (ESCAP) of 176 prostituted children in six countries, HIV infection rates ranged from 5% in Vietnam to 17% in Thailand. According to another report, 50–90% of children rescued from brothels in parts of southeast Asia are infected with HIV. The risk of HIV infection in prostituted children will depend on several factors, including the local prevalence of HIV infection in sex workers, access to condoms, and attitudes of clients towards their use. In some communities, up to 86% of sex workers are infected with HIV. Adolescent girls have a 1% risk of acquiring HIV infection during one act of unprotected sex with an infected partner. In addition, prostituted children who are infected with an STD that causes genital ulcers, such as syphilis or chancroid, have a four times increased risk of HIV infection. Lack of clinical services for children with STDs increases their risk of acquiring HIV since they will be untreated or will self-medicate. Finally, prostituted children who are infected with HIV have a very high risk of developing active tuberculosis.

Prostituted children are at high risk of acquiring STDs other than HIV, transmitting these diseases to their infants and clients, and developing drug-resistant forms of STDs. In prostituted children in the ESCAP study, STD rates were far higher in Cambodia (36%), China (78%), and Thailand (38%) than the 5% yearly incidence of these diseases in adolescents worldwide.

Rates of STDs in adult sex workers are also high in some countries. As with HIV infection, prostituted children are at higher risk of STDs than adult sex workers in locations where they have less power to negotiate use of condoms by their clients. Without use of condoms, the risk of transmission of STDs is high; during one act of unprotected sex with an infected partner, an adolescent girl has a 30% risk of acquiring genital herpes simplex virus and a 50% risk of acquiring gonorrhoea. A serious long-term health implication of untreated STDs in prostituted female children is pelvic inflammatory disease, which can result in infertility, ectopic pregnancy, chronic pelvic pain, and an increased risk of hysterectomy.

Prostituted children may receive prophylaxis for STDs or may self-medicate, placing them at risk for developing drug-resistant strains of microbes. For example, in brothel-based sex workers in Indonesia, 89% of *Neisseria gonorrhoeae* infections were resistant to penicillin and 98% to tetracycline.

Reducing STD Transmission

Caring for prostituted children is necessary not only for their health, but also to reduce transmission of STDs within communities. In Japan, 55% of men with chlamydia urethritis and 65% of men with gonorrhoea presenting at an STD clinic had been infected by sex workers. Likewise, sex workers were identified as a key factor in the huge HIV epidemic in Thailand. In addition, the clients of sex workers further the transmission of infections in communities through infecting their partners.

Infection with the hepatitis B virus (HBV), hepatitis C virus (HCV), or both is a serious health risk for prostituted children. For example, in Brazil, 18 (2.7%) of 645 sex workers were infected with HBV and 12 (2.5%) of 464 were infected with HCV. As with STDs, prostituted children can also infect their clients and third-party contacts with HBV and HCV.

Cervical cancer has been causally linked with infection with human papillomavirus. Women's risk of developing cervical cancer is associated with a high number of sexual partners and young age at first intercourse. Prostituted girls, therefore, have an increased risk of cervical cancer; they also have a high risk of being diagnosed at an advanced stage of disease, for which successful treatment is less likely.

As a result of poor living conditions, prostituted children may be at increased risk of other infectious diseases, such as tuberculosis, hepatitis A, skin infections, and parasitic infestations.

A High-Risk Group

Pregnancy

"Given the identified risks for child bearing at a young maternal age (ie, poor nutrition, substance abuse, and lack of prenatal care), it is difficult to find a risk group to which these young women do not belong".

From a study in pregnant prostituted adolescents in the USA.

Sexually active adolescents who do not use contraception have a 90% chance of becoming pregnant within 1 year. Since many prostituted girls do not have access to contraceptives, many will become pregnant. These girls are also at high risk of pregnancy-related complications, including death. Although there are no specific data on pregnancy-related morbidity and mortality in prostituted children or adult sex workers, maternal morbidity in girls younger than 18 years is two to five times greater than in women aged 18–25 years, and pregnancy-related deaths resulting from obstructed labour, infections, haemorrhage, abortion, and anaemia, are the leading cause of death for girls aged 15–19 years worldwide.

Many prostituted children who become pregnant seek abortions: in the ESCAP study, of 12 girls who became pregnant in Vietnam, eight had abortions. Between 1.0 and 4.4 million abortions are done on adolescents every year, many of which are unsafe. These abortions place prostituted children at high risk of death and injury. Of an estimated 20 million unsafe abortions done every year, 80,000 result in maternal deaths—nearly 13% of all maternal deaths. In addition, between 10% and 50% of all women who undergo unsafe abortions require medical care for complications.

Mental illness Child prostitution often results in serious long-term psychological harm, including anxiety, depression, and behavioural disorders. For example, in a study [of] 12 sex workers in Cambodia, all the women and girls had been victimised and felt helpless, damaged, degraded, betrayed, and shamed. Many of the young women reported depression, hopelessness, inability to sleep, nightmares, poor appetite, and a sense of resignation.

Prostituted children are also at high risk of suicide and post-traumatic stress disorder. In the USA, 25 (41%) of 61 pregnant prostituted adolescents reported that they had seriously considered or attempted suicide within the past year. 67% of 475 sex workers in five countries met the diagnostic criteria for post-traumatic stress disorder. Such mental health problems are serious challenges to effective treatment and re-integration of these children into society.

Substance abuse Based on rates of substance abuse by sex workers of nearly 100% in some locations, a high percentage of prostituted children probably abuse various substances from tobacco and alcohol to inhalants and opiates, incurring health risks such as overdose; permanent kidney, liver, and brain damage; infection with HIV, HBV, HCV, and other bloodborne infections; and cancer.

Violence Prostituted children are at risk of injuries, including rape, as a result of violence from pimps, clients, police, and intimate partners. Girls who are forced into prostitution may be physically and emotionally abused into submission. Other girls are beaten to induce miscarriages. Results from a study of 475 prostitutes in five countries underscore their risk of violence-related injuries. 73% of participants reported being physically assaulted while working as a sex worker, and 62% reported having been raped since entering prostitution. Children can be killed by such violence. In the USA, 27 sex workers, of whom at least two were children, have been murdered since 1997. In a study based in London, UK [United Kingdom], two of 320 sex workers had been murdered, a death rate six times the expected rate for women of similar age who are not sex workers.

Malnutrition Although malnutrition has been reported in prostituted children, especially those living on the street, no specific data on malnutrition in sex workers were available for estimating its effect. However, considering the poor living conditions of many of these children, they are probably at risk of malnutrition and related disorders.

The Children of Children

Health of infants born to prostituted children Almost no data exist on the health of infants born to prostituted children or adult sex workers. Only one report, from the USA, provides mortality data for infants born to prostituted girls. Four (8%) of 55 infants born during the study died, and 38 (67%) were referred to child protection agencies. The situation is unlikely to be better in other countries. Interviews by one of the authors (BMW) with adult sex workers and prostituted children in Pakistan and Rwanda revealed that few mothers received prenatal care or had their infants immunised against common infectious diseases. Infants born to prostituted girls are at risk of HIV, HBV, and HCV infections. An estimated 600,000 children worldwide are infected with HIV every year, most through transmission from their mothers. Interventions can reduce the risk of mother-to-child HIV transmission, but there is no prenatal intervention to reduce HCV transmission through the same mechanism. In addition, fetuses or infants may be harmed if the mother is infected with an STD. For example, congenital syphilis is a primary cause of neonatal death and morbidity in some countries.

Comprehensive quantitative studies on child prostitution are urgently needed at community, national, and global levels to assess the magnitude of child prostitution, identify the conditions under which children are forced into prostitution, identify the health problems of these children, and determine the long-term health needs of children who are no longer prostituted. Data from these studies could be used to develop interventions to prevent child prostitution; mitigate the health problems of prostituted children; and develop effective approaches to remove children from prostitution, assist them in their recovery, and reintegrate them into society. Research could also assist in identification and quantification of the health risks incurred by children who are trafficked for prostitution. Finally, we need to understand how to prevent exploitation of children by clients and why some clients target children, despite existing laws.

"Male prostitutes start work at an earlier age than females, and young prostitutes tend to engage in a lot of high-risk behaviors."

Male Prostitutes Face Numerous Risks

Peter McKnight

Male prostitutes have a lot in common with their female counterparts but face greater risks, argues Peter McKnight in the following viewpoint. According to McKnight, studies show that both male and female prostitutes have often been sexually abused. Unlike female prostitutes, however, male sex workers are often homosexual and are forced into the streets after leaving home because they are not accepted. Male prostitutes are also at higher risk of contracting HIV than female prostitutes because they often begin sex work at a younger age and take more risks. Mc-Knight is an editor of the Vancouver Sun.

As you read, consider the following questions:

1. According to McKnight, what is the primary focus of the discussion over prostitution?
2. What does the author claim is important to remember as young people face a barrage of antigay rhetoric?
3. According to the author, what do many HIV studies confirm?

Peter McKnight, "Sexual Safety and Stereotypes," *Vancouver Sun*, September 20, 2003. p. C7. Reproduced by permission.

Men of the night might be invisible, but they face danger and disease too.

A father and son are in a car accident. The father is killed and the boy is seriously injured, in need of immediate surgery. After the boy is rushed to the hospital, the surgeon exclaims, "I can't operate on him—he's my son!"

So what is the surgeon's exact relationship to the boy?

The answer, of course, is that the surgeon is his mother. That was a cutting-edge riddle back in the 1970s, when few people ever thought of women being surgeons.

The Gendering of Jobs

The riddle reveals a simple, but unacknowledged, truth: We all have theories about the world, and those theories influence what we observe or fail to observe. If our theory says all surgeons are men, then we will be completely oblivious to the female surgeons in our midst.

While most North Americans have now incorporated the notion of female surgeons into their world view, we continue to view many professions as either male or female. This "gendering" of jobs is most evident when it comes to the world's oldest profession: prostitution.

We've been hearing a lot about prostitution lately. . . .

But amidst all the chatter, we've not heard a word from, or about, men involved in prostitution. All discussions have thus far focused on how prostitution laws affect women on the street and what we can do to protect those women. Those are undeniably important discussions, but they suggest that we view prostitution as the exclusive domain of women.

In fact, though men of the night might be invisible, they're far from non-existent. In the late 1980s, the department of justice estimated that about 25 per cent of all prostitutes were men or boys. That estimate is likely low, however, because it was based on arrest statistics. Male prostitutes get arrested much less frequently than female sex workers, because police officers tend to avoid male prostitutes at all costs.

More reliable studies, including one conducted in Ottawa in 1994 and one in Victoria in 1997, have found that men and boys comprise about half of all sex-trade workers.

And that's not the only way in which male prostitutes have achieved equality with their female counterparts. The causes of prostitution—particularly physical and sexual abuse—are disconcertingly egalitarian in their application to both male and female sex-trade workers.

The sexual abuse of boys is much higher than is commonly thought, and that abuse often contributes to boys leaving home at a young age and ending up in the sex trade. A 1996 Vancouver study discovered that 51 per cent of male prostitutes had been subject to sexual abuse, compared to 31 per cent (still an astonishingly high figure) of men not involved in the sex trade.

Facing Unique Pressures

Though male and female prostitutes share much in common, boys face some unique pressures, particularly in relation to sexuality. The Badgley Committee, a comprehensive study of child sexual abuse and juvenile prostitution in Canada, discovered that only 23 per cent of male prostitutes describe themselves as heterosexual.

Many homosexual prostitutes say they left home at a young age because they were unable to find acceptance at home or at school. That means societal attitudes have played a significant role in pushing these boys onto the streets. That's something to remember as young people currently face a barrage of anti-gay rhetoric on a daily basis, thanks to the continuing, acrimonious debate about same-sex marriage.

Once on the street, male prostitutes also face risks not shared equally by women. According to the Badgley Committee, male sex workers who engage in homosexual prostitution face significantly higher risks of contracting HIV than do female prostitutes.

From Abuse to Selling Sex

Steven has been selling sex for the past four years. He says he does so because it allows him to buy expensive clothes, go to the best restaurants and have a lifestyle which makes it appear he is in control of his life.

He thinks that what he does now, at 18, is not so different [than] what happened when he was a child, when his stepfather, after repeatedly abusing him sexually, took him to the homes of friends. There, in exchange for sex, he was given gifts and treats. So there was no sudden transition, no major lifestyle choice involved; he simply performed as he had been taught.

The costs have been enormous.

Mike George, Guardian, *July 4, 2001*

That risk is compounded by the fact that male prostitutes start work at an earlier age than females, and young prostitutes tend to engage in a lot of high-risk behaviours.

Many studies have confirmed the relationship between male prostitution and HIV. In 1993, the Hospital for Sick Children in Toronto studied 700 street youth of both sexes and found that of the 16 youth testing positive for HIV, 15 were male sex workers. A similar study of 641 street youth in Montreal in 1996 discovered that 12 of 13 HIV-positive youth were boy prostitutes.

Given the prevalence and problems of male prostitution, it's surprising that male sex workers remain invisible to most people. And if federal committees and community forums are similarly unaware of male prostitution, then any solutions they offer will be half solutions, because they'll only address half of the problem.

Periodical Bibliography

The following articles have been selected to supplement the diverse views presented in this chapter.

Chris Beyrer   "Is Trafficking a Health Issue?" *Lancet*, February 14, 2004.

Helen Epstein   "The Hidden Cause of AIDS," *New York Review of Books*, May 9, 2002.

Bay Fang   "Young Lives for Sale," *U.S. News & World Report*, October 24, 2005.

John Gibb   "Sex and Slavery," *Observer*, February 23, 2003.

Lisa Katayama   "Sex Trafficking: Zero Tolerance," *Mother Jones*, May 4, 2005.

Nicholas D. Kristof   "Leaving the Brothel Behind," *Liberal Opinion Week*, February 7, 2005.

Peter Landesman   "The Girls Next Door," *New York Times Magazine*, January 25, 2004.

Tracy Quan   "Green River Killings Point up Prostitutes' Plight," *San Francisco Chronicle*, December 28, 2003.

Nina Shapiro   "The New Abolitionists," *Seattle Weekly*, August 25–31, 2004.

Richard Tyler   "Child Trafficking in Eastern Europe: A Trade in Human Misery," World Socialist Web Site, October 25, 2003. www.wsws.org

Cathy Young   "Was Story About Sexual Trafficking Exaggerated?" *Boston Globe*, February 9, 2004.

OPPOSING
VIEWPOINTS®
SERIES

CHAPTER 2

How Should Society View Prostitution?

Chapter Preface

One of several controversies in the debate over how society should view prostitution is whether prostitution should be considered "sex work." Some claim that labeling prostitution sex work will improve the lives of prostitutes. Others argue that such labels only further harm prostitutes.

Those who believe that prostitution should be regarded as sex work contend that this characterization will provide prostitutes with the protections afforded other workers. If prostitution is considered labor, they reason, national and international laws that protect workers from exploitation and other abuses can be used to protect prostitutes. Jo Bindman of Anti-Slavery International maintains, "By looking at commercial sex as work, and at the conditions under which that work is performed, sex workers can be included and protected under the existing instruments which aim to protect all workers in a general way." When prostitution is viewed as a crime, these analysts argue, the resulting outcast status of prostitutes denies them the protection of laws that are available to others. "This social exclusion renders the prostitute vulnerable to exploitation," claims Bindman. "Their predicament is made much worse ... by the stigma and criminal charges widely attached to prostitution, which allow police and other officials to harass them without ever intervening to uphold their most elementary rights," she asserts. Nor does viewing prostitution as a human rights violation erase the stigma of prostitution, these commentators claim; well-intentioned attempts to make criminals of pimps and brothel owners, rather than prostitutes, only exacerbate the problem. Laws that label pimps and brothel owners as criminals underscore the difference between prostitutes and other workers. Indeed, argues Bindman, it "emphasizes the distinction between prostitutes and other forms of female or low-status labour, such as cleaning or food-serving, however exploitative they are. It thus reinforces the marginal, and therefore vulnerable, position of the women and men involved in prostitution."

Other analysts disagree. Labeling prostitution as sex work is the real threat to prostitutes, they argue. Prostitution promotes inequality, they assert, and labeling it sex work simply institutionalizes these inequalities. Women whose status in society has forced them into prostitution do not want to be accepted as legitimate workers, these analysts contend; they want a way out. According to Janice G. Raymond, co-executive director of the Coalition Against Trafficking in Women, "Many progressives . . . are out of touch with the majority of women in prostitution who want not 'better working conditions' but a better life." Analysts such as Raymond believe that prostitution is a crime—a human rights violation. "Prostitution," Raymond argues, "is not 'sex work,' it is violence against women. It exists because significant numbers of men are given social, moral and legal permission to buy women on demand. It exists because pimps and traffickers prey on women's poverty and inequality. It exists because it is a last ditch survival strategy, not a choice, for millions of the world's women." Moreover, likeminded analysts maintain, calling prostitution sex work does not reduce the harm to prostitutes. The exact opposite is often true. Citing a study on the impact of legalization in Australia, Alice Leuchtag maintains:

> Legalization in Australia has perpetuated and strengthened the culture of violence and exploitation inherent in prostitution. Under legalization, legal and illegal brothels have proliferated, and trafficking in women has accelerated to meet the increased demand. Pimps, having even more power, continue threatening and brutalizing the women they control. Buyers continue to abuse women, refuse to wear condoms, and spread the HIV virus—and other sexually transmitted diseases—to their wives and girlfriends. Stigmatized by identity cards and medical inspections, prostituted women are even more marginalized and tightly locked into the system

of organized sexual exploitation while the state, now an official party to the exploitation, has become the biggest pimp of all.

Whether identifying prostitution as sex work will improve the status and well-being of prostitutes or will lead to the institutionalized abuse of women remains controversial. How societies view prostitution is important because attitudes shape the policies that govern the practice. The authors in the following chapter debate how society should view prostitution in order to best protect women.

> "The criminal law is likely to continue to ban prostitution, an institution against which marriage wishes to define itself."

Society Views Prostitution as a Crime

Sherry F. Colb

Prostitution is illegal in order to protect the institution of marriage, claims Rutgers University law professor Sherry F. Colb in the following viewpoint. Although most consider marriage a mutual, loving relationship, many married women provide sex in exchange for financial support, argues Colb. Because prostitution is also an exchange of sex for money, she asserts, governments ban prostitution to distinguish marriage from prostitution.

As you read, consider the following questions:

1. In Colb's opinion, what is it about an offense that makes shaming an effective punishment?

2. Under what circumstances is the U.S. Supreme Court willing to defer to state legislatures, in the author's view?

3. How does the author describe traditional marriage?

Sherry F. Colb, "What a Shame: Oakland Announces Plans to Post Photos of Convicted Johns," *FindLaw's Writ*, March 2, 2005. Copyright © 2005 FindLaw, a Thomson business. This column originally appeared on FindLaw.com. Reproduced by permission.

[In February 2005] Oakland [California] City Council President Ignacio De La Fuente announced plans to post pictures of convicted johns—people found guilty of soliciting prostitutes—on billboards and bus stops. Such a penalty raises a variety of questions.

One question concerns the proper role of shaming in our criminal justice system. . . .

Another asks about the comparative culpability of johns and prostitutes, the latter of whom ordinarily bear the brunt of any criminal sanctions against the practice.

And a third addresses a larger issue—namely, why the so-called oldest profession is against the law at all. In this column, I will turn my attention to that final question.

Posting Photographs Is an Effective Punishment

One way of approaching the matter is to ask why shaming works. That is, why would many men find it mortifying to have their pictures posted on billboards as solicitors or customers of prostitutes? A number of possible answers suggest themselves.

Perhaps being convicted of any crime is embarrassing, and therefore, almost everyone would be ashamed to be publicly identified as a criminal. There may be some truth to this. Still, it is unlikely that a conviction for driving over the speed limit or [jay]-walking would be nearly as stigmatizing. It is therefore something about the content of the particular offense involved that accounts for the effectiveness of shaming as a punitive measure.

A second possibility is that soliciting a prostitute is a terrible crime akin to murder or rape, and that is what accounts for the shame. But that too seems implausible.

Many people view prostitution as a victimless crime precisely because it is *not* inherently a terrible thing. Assuming

67

that the prostitute is an adult, no one necessarily gets hurt, and everyone arguably gets a benefit.

Granted, Oakland residents choose to inflict shaming penalties because the presence of prostitutes walking around a neighborhood can depress property values and strikes many as contributing to a sleazy atmosphere. But such opposition might as easily form in response to efforts to place a group home for mentally retarded adults in a neighborhood, and there is nothing terrible about mentally retarded people. The truth is that anything un-glamorous could drive down property values without in any way violating a criminal law or a norm against evil behavior.

So what accounts for the shame?

A likely answer is the societal perception that people who have to pay another person to have sex with them must be undesirable. This perception may be accurate as to some johns, while others may go to prostitutes to avoid the emotional entanglements that frequently result from uncompensated sexual relations. Still others may wish to live out sexual fantasies that the women (or men) in their lives find unappealing.

Why Prostitution Is a Crime

But why are prostitution and solicitation *against the law*?

Regardless of whether the perception of johns as sexually desperate is accurate, this appearance cannot account for the criminal status of solicitation. Being undesirable to people of the opposite (or same) sex can be embarrassing, in the way that being viewed as a "loser" in high school is embarrassing. But it is no crime. So how could behavior that merely evidences that reality be criminal?

The simple explanation for why prostitution is a crime is that it is a morals offense—a sin. Though neither party to the transaction is necessarily harmed, the law here prohibits sexual activity that falls outside of the prescribed relations.

But doesn't this explanation prove too much? Wouldn't an opposition to "sinful" sexual relations extend to homosexual contacts, nonprocreative forms of heterosexual sex, and fornication as well? Yes, it would.

But the Supreme Court has already said of homosexual relations, in *Lawrence v. Texas*, that a right of privacy protects against state intervention in the form of criminal penalties. Is prostitution the next practice to be protected by the Court?

Not likely. Though prostitution is currently legal in Nevada, every other state categorically prohibits it, and the Supreme Court rarely invalidates such widely shared criminal prohibitions. The trend in the case of homosexuality laws had already favored decriminalization, while no such trend characterizes the law regarding prostitution. Furthermore, the Court has been especially willing to defer to legislatures when they take aim at commercial practices—and prostitution, of course, involves commerce.

Boundary-Enforcing Prohibitions

But what explains the continuing near-universal criminalization of prostitution, even as bans on other "sinful" sexual practices have begun to disappear? What is so special about prostitution? The paradox here may be precisely that prostitution is not "special." It may, in other words, be the resemblance between the commercial practice of prostitution and permissible sexual behavior, rather than the distinctions between them, that make prostitution a target of the criminal law. In that sense, prohibitions against prostitution are boundary-enforcing prohibitions.

Consider the traditional marriage. The bride's father pays a dowry to the groom or his family for taking on the burden of providing financial support for the bride. Marrying "well," in fact, is still understood to mean that one's chosen has a lot of money or assets, which will now become property of both partners.

In exchange for financial support, traditionally, the bride will become available to the groom sexually and will bear him children and take care of his home. Though the exchange includes much more than sex, it does quite plainly contemplate that sex will be provided for the man, and that money will be provided for the woman.

It is in part for this reason that most states did not recognize marital rape as a criminal offense until relatively recently. By marrying, a man was understood to have purchased a season pass to sexual favors from his wife.

The law has in many respects evolved, and marital rape is now virtually everywhere a crime (though frequently one that receives more lenient treatment than other rapes). Furthermore, women, as well as men, have acknowledged sexual desires that they seek to meet when they marry. At the same time, most women currently work outside the home and therefore do not depend for their survival upon support from their husbands in the way that a child would from her parents. Reciprocity, in other words, has begun to replace exchange as the currency of marriage.

Marriage's Implicit Barter of Sex for Money

Despite the changes, however, studies suggest that women continue to prefer less frequent sexual interaction than their husbands do, and that men continue to earn more money than their wives, a disparity that becomes especially pronounced once a couple has children. Thus, the exchange of sex for money within marriage has not disappeared, even with the fading of traditional marital role assignments.

That exchange, however, is and always has been obscured by the many other items traded as well. One might think of the provision of money for sex within marriage, then, as more of a barter phenomenon than an outright purchase.

Prostitution, by contrast, rips away the veneer and makes explicitly commercial what might otherwise be viewed as mu-

The Legal Frameworks Governing Prostitution

Prohibition. The act of accepting payment for sex and sometimes paying for sex is illegal and punished. This is the situation, for example, in the Gulf States and in most of the United States.

Criminalization. The law forbids certain activities related to payment for sex rather than paid sex itself. These activities include soliciting for clients, advertising, living off the earnings of prostitutes, recruiting prostitutes or helping them to circulate from one country to another. This is the most common legal framework for commercial sex throughout Western Europe, India, Southeast Asia, Canada, Australia and the Pacific and most of Latin America.

Regulation refers to exceptions to criminal law made for those parts of the sex industry which comply with certain conditions. In the case of female sex workers, such systems are often linked to mandatory health checks.

UNESCO Courier, *December 1998*

tually desired. The prostitute takes money and provides a sexual service for that money. There is no love . . ., and there is no promise of continuing exchange. It is akin to the sale of a carton of apple juice, in contrast to a relational contract between ongoing businesses.

Many would rather not think of married people as exchanging sex for money. Married couples are in love and share both sex and money out of affection and commitment and mutual desire, rather than an interest in compensation. For couples for whom this picture is true, prostitution is no threat at all. It is an entirely different practice that looks nothing like what they have.

But for couples for whom mutuality is an illusion, the existence of prostitution is an unattractive mirror that puts the lie to marriage's pretensions.

When prostitutes are asked why they do what they do, they often respond that they feel freer than wives who must provide sex and so much more to their husbands in return for financial support. Prostitutes thus view what wives do for their husbands as simply a more encumbered version of what they do for their clients.

As time goes on, we can hope that every marriage will become a friendship between lovers who want the same things out of life. But the reality for many marriages is far more the market exchange model that characterizes prostitution, though for a longer term.

As long as this is true, the criminal law is likely to continue to ban prostitution, an institution against which marriage wishes to define itself.

| "Prostitution may be a grubby business,
  but it's not the government's."

Society Should Not View Prostitution as a Crime

Economist

In the following viewpoint the editors of the Economist, *a British newsmagazine, argue that prostitution is not a crime but a private transaction between two people. Prostitution is not inherently harmful, the authors maintain. Indeed, few women are forced into prostitution and studies claiming all prostitutes are victims of sexual and drug abuse are flawed, they assert. Moreover, the authors contend that legalization would decrease rather than increase any harms associated with prostitution, such as disease and drug abuse.*

As you read, consider the following questions:

1. According to the *Economist*, when do most governments even bother with prostitution?

2. Why are many of the rich world's prostitutes foreigners, in the authors' view?

3. In the authors' opinion, how has legalized prostitution failed to fulfill detractors' greatest fears?

Two adults enter a room, agree [on] a price, and have sex. Has either committed a crime? Common sense suggests not: sex is not illegal in itself, and the fact that money has changed hands does not turn a private act into a social menace. If both parties consent, it is hard to see how either is a victim. But prostitution has rarely been treated as just another transaction, or even as a run-of-the-mill crime: the oldest profession is also the oldest pretext for outraged moralising and unrealistic lawmaking devised by man.

In recent years, governments have tended to bother with prostitution only when it threatened public order. Most countries (including Britain and America) have well-worn laws against touting on street corners, against the more brazen type of brothel and against pimping. This has never been ideal, partly because sellers of sex feel the force of law more strongly than do buyers, and partly because anti-soliciting statutes create perverse incentives. On some occasions, magistrates who have fined streetwalkers have been asked to wait a few days so that the necessary money can be earned.

So there is perennial discussion of reforming prostitution laws. During the 1990s, the talk was all of liberalisation. Now the wind is blowing the other way. In 1999, Sweden criminalised the buying of sex. France then cracked down on soliciting and outlawed commercial sex with vulnerable women—a category that includes pregnant women. Britain began to enforce new laws against kerb-crawling earlier this year, and is now considering more restrictive legislation. Outside a few pragmatic enclaves, attitudes are hardening. Whereas, ten years ago, the discussion was mostly about how to manage prostitution and make it less harmful, the aim now is to find ways to stamp it out.

The puritans have the whip hand not because they can prove that tough laws will make life better for women, but because they have convinced governments that prostitution is intolerable by its very nature. What has tipped the balance is the globalisation of the sex business.

The White Slave Trade

It is not surprising that many of the rich world's prostitutes are foreigners. Immigrants have a particularly hard time finding jobs that pay well; local language skills are not prized in the sex trade; prostitutes often prefer to work outside their home town. But the free movement of labour is as controversial in the sex trade as in any other business. Wherever they work, foreign prostitutes are accused of driving down prices, touting "extra" services and consorting with organised criminal pimps who are often foreigners, too. The fact that a very small proportion of women are trafficked—forced into prostitution against their will—has been used to discredit all foreigners in the trade, and by extension (since many sellers of sex are indeed foreign) all prostitutes.

Abolitionists make three arguments. From the right comes the argument that the sex trade is plain wrong, and that, by condoning it, society demeans itself. Liberals ... who believe that what consenting adults do in private is their own business reject that line.

From the left comes the argument that all prostitutes are victims. Its proponents cite studies that show high rates of sexual abuse and drug taking among employees. To which there are two answers. First, those studies are biased: they tend to be carried out by staff at drop-in centres and by the police, who tend to see the most troubled streetwalkers. Taking their clients as representative of all prostitutes is like assessing the state of marriage by sampling shelters for battered women. Second, the association between prostitution and drug addiction does not mean that one causes the other: drug addicts, like others, may go into prostitution just because it's a good way of making a decent living if you can't think too clearly.

Turning Some Women into Criminals

If we, as a society, really care about women, we will not only provide them with equal rights and opportunity, but we will stop turning some of them into criminals merely because they have chosen to exchange sex for money. Women, who, for whatever reason, choose to engage in prostitution, do not need to be incarcerated for their own good.

Edward Tabash, Los Angeles Times, *August 11, 1993.*

A third, more plausible, argument focuses on the association between prostitution and all sorts of other nastinesses, such as drug addiction, organised crime, trafficking and underage sex. To encourage prostitution, goes the line, is to encourage those other undesirables; to crack down on prostitution is to discourage them.

Brothels with Brands

Plausible, but wrong. Criminalisation forces prostitution into the underworld. Legalisation would bring it into the open, where abuses such as trafficking and under-age prostitution can be more easily tackled. Brothels would develop reputations worth protecting. Access to health care would improve—an urgent need, given that so many prostitutes come from diseased parts of the world. Abuses such as child or forced prostitution should be treated as the crimes they are, and not discussed as though they were simply extreme forms of the sex trade, which is how opponents of prostitution and, recently, the governments of Britain and America have described them.

Puritans argue that where laws have been liberalised—in, for instance, the Netherlands, Germany and Australia—the new regimes have not lived up to claims that they would wipe out pimping and sever the links between prostitution and organised crime. Certainly, those links persist; but that's because, thanks to concessions to the opponents of liberalisation, the changes did not go far enough. Prostitutes were made to register, which many understandably didn't want to do. Not surprisingly, illicit brothels continued to thrive.

If those quasi-liberal experiments have not lived up to their proponents' expectations, they have also failed to fulfil their detractors' greatest fears. They do not seem to have led to outbreaks of disease or under-age sex, nor to a proliferation of street prostitution, nor to a wider collapse in local morals.

Which brings us back to that discreet transaction between two people in private. If there's no evidence that it harms others, then the state should let them get on with it. People should be allowed to buy and sell whatever they like, including their own bodies. Prostitution may be a grubby business, but it's not the government's.

"The conditions in which prostitution is practised are such as to violate explicitly the respect and dignity of the person."

Prostitution Should Be Seen as Degrading

Elaine Audet

In the following viewpoint feminist poet and writer Elaine Audet contends that prostitutes are marketable merchandise that men can abuse with impunity. Prostitutes do not freely use their bodies for their own benefit, she argues. In fact, Audet claims, most prostitutes would leave prostitution if they could. Indeed, viewing prostitution as just another form of work ignores the reality that pimps and brothel owners benefit from prostitution at the expense of prostitutes. Liberalization of prostitution does not help prostitutes, Audet asserts, it merely condones the degradation of women.

As you read, consider the following questions:

1. In Audet's view, what do all studies about prostitution demonstrate?
2. According to the author, why are most girls recruited for prostitution at age thirteen?
3. What message do assaulted prostitutes who do not lodge a complaint send, in the author's view?

Elaine Audet, "Prostitution: Rights of Women or Right to Women?" http://Sisyphe.org, September 14, 2002. Reproduced by permission.

Since the seventies, there has been a trend towards recognition of the concept of "sex workers" in Quebec, Europe and the United States. Viewing prostitutes as "sex workers" suggests that they are merely labourers providing a "social" service and should be given, therefore, the same rights as other exploited workers who are crushed by the forces of globalisation, and turned into marketable objects.

In Quebec, members of Stella [a Montreal prostitute rights' group] have spoken the loudest in favour of the liberalisation of prostitution. They reject the idea that prostitutes should be treated as victims and say that most prostitutes have freely chosen this role, finding in their work a source of empowerment. No doubt, prostitutes have great courage. Testimonies from these women, such as that in Jeanne Cordelier's memoirs of prostitution, highlight this: "When the door of the room bangs, there's no escape. . . . Dead end, no emergency exit." But despite this courage, and the claims of Stella, there is room for scepticism, especially when data from an international study show that 92% of the prostitutes would leave prostitution if they could.

A Gradual Slide Toward Dehumanisation

In debates about prostitution, all words are loaded, in particular the concepts of rights, free choice, sexual workers. Concerning the latter, for example, the French ex-prostitute, Agnès Laury, believes that seeing these women as "merchandise sold by men to men" would be closer to their reality.

We live in a consumerist/consuming society where priority goes to individualism and to the unrestrained consumption of people and things, the ne plus ultra becoming for us to consume one another. In such a context, viewing prostitutes as sex workers erases feminist opposition to the marketing of women on a global scale. It allows the johns to assert that women do this by "choice," even by "taste," thereby hiding what all studies demonstrate: that women prostitute themselves out of necessity.

Patriarchal culture rests on the principle that the unique duty, and source of power, of women is to satisfy men sexually in marriage or by prostitution. The existence of prostitution, and viewing it as "sex work," hides the extent of this sexual slavery and reinforces the notion that women are simply interchangeable objects that must be accessible and ready for all men at all time and everywhere.

The Interests at Stake

When we consider who would profit from the liberalisation of prostitution, it becomes clear that it would NOT be prostitutes or women in general. Rather, the beneficiaries will be pimps, dealers, organised crime, customers, and all those who view sexuality as but a mechanical act, deprived of reciprocity and of any responsibility. Liberalisation will only benefit those, whatever their social status, who want to be able to purchase power over a woman.

Of course, it is impossible to speak about prostitutes as a whole; their situations will differ considerably according to whether they are call girls, escorts, or nude dancers; whether they work on the streets or in massage salons; whether they are autonomous, or must give most of the money they earn to a pimp.

Girls are often recruited for prostitution at about age thirteen when many of them have been made vulnerable by violence, poverty, unemployment, and drugs in the environments where they live. The majority have experienced forced dressage by pimps or members of street gangs who seek to depersonalise a woman until she loses the ability to act on her own initiative or even to think for herself. Many girls have spent time in shelters, reform houses or prisons; more than half are drug addicts. Living in and experiencing such circumstances, how can one talk about a girl's/woman's free choice to prostitute?

On an international scale, revenues from prostitution are about $72 billion a year, now more lucrative than the traffic in weapons and drugs. This translates into millions of dollars in Canada, where a pimp collects on average $144,000 a year from each of his prostitutes. Although, 5,000 to 10,000 persons in Montreal make their living in the prostitution business, many others have some interest in the expansion of such a profitable market. And given their connections, these potential prostitution-profiteers have the financial and media resources to deflect legitimate critique of prostitution and to exaggerate the importance of division within the feminist movement by adopting the position of a "free choice" minority who pretends to speak for all prostitutes. In so doing, they mostly only support liberalisation to retain their own control.

The Merchandised Body

The present movement for the liberalisation of prostitution is rooted in the general movement to liberalise trade, and serves this neo-liberal approach by framing prostitution as "good" for the economy. Thus, in the media and at the UN [United Nations], there is an increasing tendency to present the sex industry as a solution to economic problems or, even more, as a road toward development.

In this regard, it is of interest that the UN-based International Labor Organization (ILO) promoted a 1998 report that supported the legalisation of prostitution because: "the possibility of an official recognition would be extremely useful for extending the taxation net to cover many of the lucrative activities connected with it." This position is clearly an admission that sex is an industry and that it can contribute directly and indirectly, and in extensive ways, to employment, national income, and economic growth.

A Violation of Human Dignity

There are solid reasons why prostitution should be illegal—for the well-being of the individual as well as of society. Prostitution is fundamentally immoral because it is inherently a violation of dignity of the human person and has been recognized as such in all times, all places and all cultures. It violates the marital union, which is the basis of our society; and it unavoidably endangers public health. The institution of sex-for-hire harms the rights and dignity of all women because it institutionalizes the principle that men have a right to turn other human beings into objects of use for the satisfaction of their lust.

Wendy Wright, Concerned Women for America, June 12, 2001.

Prostitution constitutes one of the most violent forms of collective oppression of women and, with but a few exceptions, it is always under the coercive control of pimps. Therefore, how can we invoke the free use of one's own body as a human right when the conditions in which prostitution is practised are such as to violate explicitly the respect and dignity of the person recognised by the Convention for the "Repression of traffic in human beings and the exploitation of someone else's prostitution," adopted December 2nd 1949 by the United Nations?

Many prostitutes, breaking the general "law of silence" enveloping them, have spoken out about their constant exposure to all kinds of humiliations, physical and sexual aggression, and theft, as well as to the "Russian roulette" of forced sexual relations without condoms or other protections. And even if not all men are violent, those seeking sex with a prostitute necessarily buy the power to be violent with impunity. "I was afraid, conscious that the situation could become uncontrollable at any moment", says a prostitute from Quebec. Moreover, [she says,] "The beaten girls who do not lodge a complaint have integrated the message society is sending back to them that prostitution is a package deal . . . that one must accept even the unacceptable." For how long will the right of men continue to be systematically confused with Human Rights?

Many arguing for the total liberalisation of prostitution try to discredit feminists who are opposed to this position by saying the latter are moralising their discourses, thereby victimising and stigmatising prostitutes. Nevertheless, the neo-abolitionists are not responsible for prostitutes' working conditions or for the hostility of those who see their neighbourhood transformed in an open market for women and drugs. Because we have not been able to extirpate a problem's causes, must we legitimate its consequences?

Trails for Action

No individual can remain indifferent to a problem which, in the end, concerns and touches us all. It is clear that whatever else it does, the liberalisation of prostitution (and of pimps and customers) as demanded by Stella, will not provide a real alternative to the growing misery of prostitutes and might, instead, only make things worse.

Similarly, with the Bloc Quebecois's proposition for a return to brothels, this "solution" would have the state become the principal pimp, a parallel to how the state has replaced the Mafia in provincial casinos. The example of the Netherlands shows that legalisation institutionalises and legitimates the sex "industry", lets pimps masquerade as "foremen" and legal "entrepreneurs," and rationalises the marketing of prostitutes locally or transnationally.

The only hope for improving the lot of prostitutes and ending the marketing of women resides in the example provided by Sweden which, in 1999, passed legislation that criminalised pimps and customers, but not the prostitutes. This policy led to a reduction by half in the number of prostitutes, even if it did not succeed in completely eradicating underground prostitution. However, the Swedish government continues to pursue its efforts by constantly injecting new funds for detoxification programs, for the reinsertion of prostitutes, and for educating customers. Of interest, and encouraging, is that the European Lobby of Women, comprising around 3500 groups, has urged the adoption by other governments of a position similar to that of Sweden.

The Changing Status of Prostitutes

In Quebec, there is a consensus that governments at all levels should cease acting toward prostitutes as if they were criminals and, instead, give them access to the health, social, legal, and police services they are requesting. Debates arise between groups on the subject of criminalising the customers, the pimps being already subject to Canadian laws, even if these have so far been applied only in very limited ways.

In establishing policy here, Quebec can find inspiration in the Swedish experience and in the approaches of cities such as Toronto and Vancouver where there are efforts to give prostitutes the help and protection they need, to put in place means of resistance to pimps and dealers (often the same), and to dissuade and sensitise customers. The abolition of prostitution can only be a long term objective, but we need now to question all social, economic, and sexual relations of domination, and take immediate steps to fight poverty and violence against women.

"To come out of it," says ex-prostitute Agnèes Laury, "one needs an unshakeable will not to go back on the sidewalk, to be helped and mostly to be totally cut off from the milieu". In short, to "come out of it" is to pass from the status of victim to that of "survivor", of a woman who fights. It is time for us all to break the silence about the buying of sexual services and to ask if it is not really the discretionary power of men to sexual violence that underlies prostitution, not women's choice. Analysing prostitution this way is not a matter of puritanism, but of asking fundamental ethical questions about the marketing of humans. Instead of invoking a "free choice" to sell one's body to justify prostitution, couldn't we call for the humanity principle, to a freely accepted limit on using humans as merchandise, such as was done in the face of slavery, to abolish the marketing of both sexuality and reproduction?

*"Prostitution gave me a growing con-
sciousness of my sexuality and a lot of
personal strength."*

Prostitution Should Be Seen as Empowering Some Women

Jillian Blume

*In the following viewpoint freelance writer and editor Jillian
Blume tells the stories of three women who became empowered
working as prostitutes. These women practice their trade in Hol-
land, where prostitution is legal. One woman sees prostitution as
a nurturing profession and gains confidence from helping her clients feel wanted. Another claims that prostitution is a job like
any other. The last woman, who works as a sadomasochistic
mistress, contends that helping people explore their secret desires
allows her to feel powerful.*

As you read, consider the following questions:

1. To what does Jacqueline equate working behind a window in the red-light district?
2. In what ways does Roos claim prostitution is like any
   other business?
3. Why do people go to a sadomasochistic mistress, in
   Winnifred's view?

Jacqueline, 39

Prostitution is definitely less about sex than people expect. I have always been fascinated by the interaction between a client and a prostitute, so 12 years ago, I contacted an escort agency.

My first client was a man who lived in a home for the elderly. We didn't even have intercourse; we just did some snuggling and a little touching. He kept his underwear on, and it was so cute—he played the harmonica for me and gave me a cup of tea and a hug. I thought it was wonderful just to be able to give him some warmth. It made me feel confident, adventurous, and beautiful, and it felt so me.

After that, I worked behind a window in the red-light district to get experience, but it wasn't satisfying. Men who come to the windows are there for a quickie—the sex is only 10 or 15 minutes long—and you need to get your clients out of the room as soon as possible to generate more revenue. But I would take more time than the other women, since I like to make a bit of a connection first.

I wasn't good at anonymous sex, and I believe my current clientele needs more than that from me. Sometimes I can feel a person's loneliness, and I hope I can make someone feel wanted and understood for an hour or two. In a lot of ways, prostitution is like social work. I've had clients with whom I've spent seven hours, just talking. Working in the windows was like McDonald's—men go there because they have an appetite and are hungry for a snack—but working for a brothel or escort agency is like going out for dinner. If you're there for a couple of hours, you want more than just to satisfy the appetite; you talk much more. It's a powerful experience to get people to open up in conversation.

Today, I have a few clients from a special escort agency that caters to people with mental, physical, and social disabilities. A guy who is disabled gets a lot of care and physical contact, like being washed and fed, but it's very professional contact. It's nice for a guy to have the chance to feel like a sexual being, not just a disabled person who needs care. There are many ways of helping people, but sometimes a snuggle, some undivided attention, and sex are important.

Roos, 48

When I was a student, I really needed money. I saw some newspaper ads for brothels seeking prostitutes, and I called one. The owner arranged an appointment with my first client.

For me, having sex wasn't sinful; prostitution was a way to communicate with other people and explore parts of myself I'd considered inferior. Until I did this, I had never exercised my ability to tempt men; I considered my personality and intelligence more important qualities. Prostitution gave me a growing consciousness of my sexuality and a lot of personal strength.

But I've found that the rest of the world doesn't think as positively about expressing sexuality. From the moment I started working, I was a disgraced person. Many of my friends and family don't understand my choice. People make judgments about my personality and morals—I'm supposed to be unintelligent, weak, lazy, unethical, and wicked. I started working before prostitution was legal [in Holland], and it was impossible to get a bank account, medical insurance, or a house. Even after legalization, banks had to be pressed to accept prostitutes as clients.

The price for breaking the rules in any society—about how women should behave, sexual freedom, how to manage sexuality—is being judged harshly. But I was proud to pay that price to fight for sexual freedom: the freedom to have no sex at all, to have sex with other women, to only have sex with the one you love, or to have sex with 1000 men.

I've tried to strengthen the position of the prostitute by being open about what I do. I regard my profession as a trade

Sex Workers' Declaration of Independence

We demand the right to choose sex work as an occupation;

We demand the recognition of sex work as a legitimate part of the global workforce and an emerging segment of the labor movement;

As individuals who have chosen this occupation, we demand the right to migrate freely, as sex workers;

We demand equal protection under the law, the right to freedom, to the pursuit of happiness and the right to live free of violence at the hands of vigilantes, police and state;

We demand the right to form our own organizations and to advocate on our own behalf;

We demand access to health care services, including HIV prevention and care.

Sex Workers Outreach Project, "Sex Workers Declaration of Independence," July 4, 2005. www.swop-usa.org

like any other, and I talk about my job freely among friends and acquaintances and in newspaper and radio interviews. I've also been involved in discussions run by *De Rode Draad* (The Red Thread), a Dutch organization that works to organize the prostitution business so that everyone is treated fairly.

Prostitution is like any other business in many ways. I have met a lot of dull, irritating, terrible men, but so what? I have also met a lot of kind and captivating men with fascinating stories and interesting opinions, and they have made my world very wide.

Winnifred, 38

I became a dominatrix on a dare. After a few amateur S&M[1] experiences at home, my husband and I went to a club and found out the management was searching for an assistant. He teased me that I wouldn't dare do it—but I did.

I hadn't known anything about S&M until a short time before I got married, but I quickly discovered that it's a way to help people. I'm not a psychologist, but I'm good at sensing people's secret longings. I play games such as bondage, role-playing, spanking, and exploring all kinds of fetishes with my clients, but I don't have sex with them. When people come to me, they are longing for certain feelings, especially excitement and attention. For some people, S&M is like working out: Afterward, you're relieved. Your heart is dancing. You're more open, and the world feels different. It's very rewarding to make people feel good.

The power that comes from being a mistress isn't about brute force. It's only when I sense that my client has given in because of trust that I'm in charge and in control. My job is all about feelings—I can sense when someone wants to be alone in a cage and when it's enough. It's very satisfying to sense how my "slaves" feel. It's as if I'm under their skin. If it's a good session, we share energy and trust, and they feel free in their experience.

My job is also very different from what I do at home, where I am a mother and a wife. I'm grateful to have a husband who lets me play. He understands that some people need S&M and have no place else to go; he always liked S&M himself but felt like he couldn't tell anyone until he met me. We've had some serious discussions about my work—but if he complains, I have my ways of putting him back on the right track!

---

1. Sadomasochism: deriving pleasure, especially sexual gratification, from inflicting or submitting to physical or emotional abuse.

"Choice is key here—women need to have the right and freedom to choose how to live their lives as sexual beings. This includes prostitution."

Society Should Regard Prostitution as a Choice

Kimberly Klinger

Some women choose to become prostitutes, claims Kimberly Klinger in the following viewpoint. These women should be free to earn a living as prostitutes and should be given the same protections accorded other workers, she argues. Policies should continue to prohibit forced prostitution, Klinger asserts, but such policies should not make criminals of prostitutes. Klinger was a member of the Feminist Majority Leadership Alliance while a student at Pennsylvania State University.

As you read, consider the following questions:

1. In Klinger's opinion, what has been the result of the demonization of feminists?
2. What is the result of dismissing the entire sex industry as abusive and immoral, in the author's view?
3. According to the author, what is the best choice for women?

Kimberly Klinger, "Prostitution, Humanism, and a Woman's Choice," *Humanist,* January-February 2003. Copyright © 2003 American Humanist Association. Reproduced by permission of the author.

Driving home in the early morning hours after a night out in Washington, D.C., I turn from 14th to L Street near downtown. I'm only on the street for a block before I hit the clogged artery of Massachusetts Avenue, and this particular area seems devoid of important business or commerce. Except for the prostitutes.

Almost every weekend night I can spot women walking up and down the street—sometimes between the cars and quite near to my own. They're stereo-typically wearing the tiniest slivers of fabric masquerading as dresses, swishing their hips as they teeter on high heels. I don't recall ever seeing any possible pimps nearby and wonder if these women operate independently. I wonder about a lot of things, actually. Are they happy? Are they safe? Are they making good money? Are they feminists?

A Third Wave Feminist

That last question may seem incongruous, but to me it's relevant. As a third wave feminist, I find sex and sex work to be important issues—ones which are being addressed in ways unheard of by our foremothers. We third wavers are, in many cases, the lip-gloss wearing, *BUST* magazine reading, pro-sex women of the new millennium. We have taken the liberties of the second wave and run with them, demanding even more freedom as we struggle to find our new identities in the ever-dominating patriarchy. We don't hold consciousness-raising sessions; we hold safe sex fairs. We still march on Washington, but we have punk rock bands helping us to raise the funds to get there. We're more multicultural and diverse, yet we continue to fight the white face—the opinion that feminism is a white women's movement—put upon us by the media.

We've also had to fight the awful stereotype that feminists are frigid, man-hating, anti-sex zealots. The second wave made incredible changes in how the United States deals with rape and domestic violence, and while we still have a long way to go, these issues are at least taken much more seriously. However, in the process, feminists have been labeled and demonized, thus creating a huge chasm between sexuality and feminism. Women are still the same sexual beings they always were, but to outsiders they have been considered strictly buzz-kills (no fun) or—gasp—lesbians. In 1983 [feminists] Andrea Dworkin and Catharine A. MacKinnon wrote major antipornography bills that negatively labeled feminists as anti-sex instead of pro-human rights.

In the third wave, pornography, sex, and prostitution aren't presented as black and white issues. For instance, pornography isn't simply seen as degrading sexual imagery made by men, for men. There are female filmmakers and feminist porn stars who want to reclaim their right to enjoy sexual images without violence and negativity. Sex is more widely discussed than ever and taboos are being broken every day. The third wave hopes to expand definitions of sexuality. For women to be liberated sexually, they must be able to live as they choose, to break out of narrow ideas of sexuality, to be sexual and still be respected, and essentially to be whole. Feminism and sex work aren't therefore mutually exclusive. Choice is key here—women need to have the right and freedom to choose how to live their lives as sexual beings. This includes prostitution.

A Choice for Some

Prostitution. The word normally calls to mind women down on their luck, pitied cases who walk the streets at night with little protection or rights—essentially women who have no other choice. And unfortunately this often isn't far from the truth. In the United States and worldwide many women turn to or are forced into sexual prostitution because they have limited options. But there are other situations, even in the United States, where women turn to this profession and other sex work because they want to. They are fortunate to have real choices and select this path because it suits them, while practicing prostitution safely and respectfully.

In the United States it is possible to find a number of organizations of sex workers who defend each other, work alongside international groups to decriminalize prostitution and protect prostitutes, and share the common experiences of choosing and enjoying this form of labor. There are advocacy and rights organizations, international conferences, and famous porn stars who all regard prostitution and other sex work as just that: a job and a way to earn a living. They argue that it should be treated as such—protected under the law with safety guidelines, unions, networks, and all the rest. Furthermore, taking a third wave feminist view, they maintain that women need to have the right and freedom to choose how to live their lives as sexual beings, including taking up "the world's oldest profession."

Coerced and Unprotected Prostitution

No matter what wave of feminism is applied, all feminists agree that forced, coerced, poverty-based, trafficked, and unprotected prostitution should be opposed. In countries where prostitution is illegal, such as in forty-nine of fifty states in the United States, women have no protection, socially or legally. The situation is messy at best and, at worst, violent, dangerous, and all but devoid of human rights. For example, most American prostitutes have to work for pimps or out of brothels, never seeing much of the money they have earned. If they are streetwalkers they live in fear of criminal assault or arrest—and in some cases, sexual abuse by police. They may be forced to deal with customers they are afraid of or who harm them. If they are raped, police will generally disregard their suffering, not even considering what in any other profession would be recognized as criminal assault and the forced rendering of service without pay. Beyond that, the victimized

"What do you mean, 'Not tonight, I have a headache'? You're a prostitute."

woman may even be arrested for practicing prostitution. The situation is even worse in poor countries where it is all too common for young girls to be forced into prostitution and where men from wealthier nations travel specifically to have sex with them.

Second wave feminist author MacKinnon has essentially deemed prostitution sexual slavery, arguing that the relevant laws immensely harm women, classifying them as criminals and denying them their basic civil rights. MacKinnon admits in an essay "Prostitution and Civil Rights" published in the *Michigan Journal of Gender and Law* that she isn't sure about what to do legally concerning prostitution but that international initiatives and policy responses can help to put the power back in women's hands where it belongs. Does this mean all prostitution would disappear if women had their say? Not if the numerous prostitute rights groups and their sympathizers are any indication.

Prostitute Rights

For many who have thought about this question, dismissing the entire sex industry as abusive and immoral only exacerbates existing problems and tosses the concerns of sex workers aside. Therefore many feminists, civil rights workers, and human rights activists argue for the decriminalization—not necessarily the legalization—of prostitution. Internationally, conferences are held that address decriminalization. The World Charter for Prostitutes Rights is one outcome. Created in 1985 this document is a template used by human rights groups all over the world—it makes certain basic demands abundantly clear:

1. Decriminalize all aspects of adult prostitution resulting from individual decision. This includes regulation of third parties (business managers) according to standard business codes.

2. Strongly enforce all laws against fraud, coercion, violence, child sexual abuse, child labor, rape, and racism everywhere and across national boundaries, whether or not in the context of prostitution.

3. Guarantee prostitutes all human rights and civil liberties, including the freedom of speech, travel, immigration, work, marriage, and motherhood and the right to unemployment insurance, health insurance, and housing.

4. Ensure that prostitutes' rights are protected.

5. Allow prostitutes to unionize.

Decriminalization essentially means the removal of laws against this and other forms of sex work. The Prostitutes Education Network clarifies that decriminalization is usually used to refer to total decriminalization—that is, the repeal of all laws against consensual adult sexual activity in both commercial and noncommercial contexts. This allows the individual prostitute to choose whether or not she is managed and protects her from fraud, abuse, and coercion.

By contrast the term legalization usually refers to a system of governmental regulation of prostitutes wherein prostitutes are licensed and required to work in specific ways. When Jesse Ventura was running for the Minnesota governorship in 1998 he proposed that Minnesotans should consider legalizing prostitution in order to have governmental control and keep it out of residential areas. This is the practice in Nevada, the only state in the United States where brothels are legal. Although legalization can also imply a decriminalized, autonomous system of prostitution, the reality is that in most "legalized" systems the police control prostitution with criminal codes. Laws regulate prostitutes' businesses and lives, prescribing health checks and registration of health status. According to the International Union of Sex Workers, legalized systems often include special taxes, the restriction of prostitutes to working in brothels or in certain zones, licenses, registration of prostitutes and the consequent keeping of records of each individual in the profession, and health checks which often result in punitive quarantine. This is why the World Charter for Prostitutes Rights doesn't support mandatory health checks. This may be controversial but it fits with the general idea that prostitutes' lives should be protected but not regulated. Easier and more affordable access to health clinics where prostitutes don't feel stigmatized is of greater concern to these human rights groups because compulsory checks can frighten some prostitutes and actually prevent those who are most at risk from getting necessary medical checkups. Many groups that support sex workers have sexual health and disease control as their top priorities and provide education, contraception, and health care referrals.

Prostitution in the Netherlands

A well-known example of legalized prostitution is that which has been practiced in the Netherlands since the 1800s; however, brothels were illegal until 2000. When the ban was lifted, forced prostitution came under harsher punishment. Brothels are now required to be licensed and it is legal to organize the prostitution of another party, provided the prostitution isn't forced. According to the A. De Graaf Foundation, laws in the Netherlands now will control and regulate the exploitation of prostitution, improve the prosecution of involuntary exploitation, protect minors, protect the position of prostitutes, combat the criminal affairs related to prostitution, and combat the presence of illegal aliens in prostitution.

Designated streetwalking zones have also been established. While these aren't without their problems, they have essentially functioned as a safe community for women to work. The zones also offer the benefit of a shelter which affords prostitutes a place to meet with their colleagues, talk to health care professionals, and generally relax. This was a good solution for an occupation that had led both police and prostitutes to feel that frequent raids were only making matters worse. Women felt scared and were always on the run, and police thought they weren't succeeding at making the streets any safer. This system of legalization seems to have worked well because in the Netherlands social attitudes about sex and sex work are more liberal than in other parts of the world. There is a genuine effort to protect and respect the rights of Dutch sex workers.

But this sort of arrangement isn't found all over the world. Nor can one say that the Netherlands example should become a model for every other country. Some societies may benefit more from decriminalization while others are decades away from any regulation whatsoever. The latter seems to be the case in the United States, where puritanical attitudes about sex in general would make it nearly impossible to treat prostitution as just another business.

The Right to Choose

What then is the best choice for women? Put simply, the best choice for women is the choice that the individual woman makes for herself. Furthermore, a humanist perspective would naturally back up the right of women to choose how to live their lives as sexual beings. Humanist Manifesto II says:

> In the area of sexuality, we believe that intolerant attitudes, often cultivated by orthodox religions and puritanical cultures, unduly repress sexual conduct. The right to birth control, abortion, and divorce should be recognized. While we do not approve of exploitive, denigrating forms of sexual expression, neither do we wish to prohibit, by law or social sanction, sexual behavior between consenting adults. The many varieties of sexual exploration should not in themselves be considered "evil." Without countenancing mindless permissiveness or unbridled promiscuity, a civilized society should be a tolerant one. Short of harming others or compelling them to do likewise, individuals should be permitted to express their sexual proclivities and pursue their lifestyles as they desire. We wish to cultivate the development of a responsible attitude toward sexuality, in which humans are not exploited as sexual objects, and in which intimacy, sensitivity, respect, and honesty in interpersonal relations are encouraged. Moral education for children and adults is an important way of developing awareness and sexual maturity.

As stated above, any variety of sexual exploration—as long as it isn't exploitative or harmful—can't be considered evil, yet that is exactly how prostitution is regarded. If a woman or man chooses to exchange sex for money and does it in a way that causes no harm to either party, then they should be free to do so.

In this new social environment, many of the prostitutes' rights groups build from the pro-sex ideals of the third wave. Groups such as COYOTE (Call Off Your Old Tired Ethics), the Blackstockings, and PONY (Prostitutes of New York) advocate for women who have chosen to be sex workers. Their websites are full of resources—from legal and medical referrals to common sense safety tips—and they advocate tirelessly for the decriminalization of prostitution.

It would seem that decriminalization should be a key point in any humanistic feminist perspective on prostitution. Every woman's choices should be legally and socially respected whether a given woman chooses to be a wife, a CEO, or a prostitute.

And what is good for women in these instances becomes good for other sex workers, such as male prostitutes, exotic dancers of both sexes, and so on—this applies to both the gay and straight communities. Furthermore, what liberates those who make sex a profession also liberates everyone else who enjoys sex recreationally. General sexiness, for example, can take on more varied and open forms—so much so that no woman would need to fear that frank sexuality in manner or dress would any longer stigmatize her as a "slut" (or if it did, the word would have lost its sting).

Feminism has always advocated for women to enjoy freedom of choice. Women have made great strides in the courtrooms, the boardrooms, and the bedrooms. But there remains a long way to go. Negative attitudes toward sexuality, in particular, have made it hard for women to be fully liberated. But thanks to feminists, prostitute activists, and their supporters, things are slowly changing. Only when women have their sexual and personal choices protected and respected can they truly be free.

> "Prostitution and trafficking can appear
> voluntary but are not really free choices
> made from a range of options."

Prostitution Is Sexual Violence

Melissa Farley

Women do not choose to become prostitutes, argues Melissa Farley in the following viewpoint. Choice implies consent, she claims, and consent requires that parties to the contract be equal, that the relationship between them is free of violence, and that all parties have realistic alternatives. Prostitutes are not on equal footing with customers and pimps; in fact, she asserts, customers and pimps coerce and control prostitutes. Moreover, prostitutes regularly experience physical abuse and even death at the hands of customers and pimps, Farley maintains. Finally, women who become prostitutes have no alternatives, Farley contends; they prostitute themselves in order to survive. Farley, a research and clinical psychologist, is editor of Prostitution, Trafficking, and Traumatic Stress.

As you read, consider the following questions:

1. According to Farley, how is prostitution like incest?

2. Of what mental disorder do prostitutes often show symptoms, in the author's view?

3. In the author's opinion, in addition to condoms and

unions, what else must organizations assisting prostitutes offer?

Sexology, the study of sexuality, was built on the uncritical acceptance of prostitution as an institution expressive of both men's and women's sexuality. Alfred C. Kinsey, Sc.D., and his colleagues worked from the 1940s through the 1970s to articulate a sexuality that was graphically portrayed in magazines. Even today, some assume that prostitution is sex. In fact, prostitution is a last-ditch means of economic survival or "paid rape," as one survivor described it. Its harms are made invisible by the idea that prostitution is sex, rather than sexual violence.

Prostitution has much in common with other kinds of violence against women. What incest is to the family, prostitution is to the community. Prostitution is widely socially tolerated and its consumers (commercial sex customers who are called johns or tricks by women in prostitution) are socially invisible.

[J.L.] Herman (2003) polled attendees at a trauma conference, asking how many currently or previously treated patients who had been used in prostitution. Three-quarters of the 600 attendees raised their hands. Describing prostitution as hidden in plain sight, Herman noted that 30 years ago, rape, domestic violence and incest were similarly invisible.

Prostitution Is Violent

Although clinicians are beginning to recognize the overwhelming physical violence in prostitution, the internal ravages of prostitution have not been well understood. Prostitution and trafficking are experiences of being hunted down, dominated, sexually harassed and assaulted. There is a lack of awareness among clinicians regarding the systematic methods of brainwashing, indoctrination and physical control that are used against women in prostitution. There has been far more clinical attention paid to sexually transmitted diseases (STDs) among those prostituted than to their depressions, lethal suicidality, mood disorders, anxiety disorders (including post-traumatic stress disorder) dissociative disorders and chemical dependence.

Regardless of prostitution's status (legal, illegal or decriminalized) or its physical location (strip club, massage parlor, street, escort/home/hotel), prostitution is extremely dangerous for women. Homicide is a frequent cause of death.

Prolonged and repeated trauma precedes entry into prostitution, with most women beginning prostitution as sexually abused adolescents. Homelessness is frequently a precipitating event to prostitution. Women in prostitution are frequently raped and physically assaulted.

Prostituted women are unrecognized victims of intimate partner violence by pimps and customers. Pimps and customers use methods of coercion and control like those of other batterers: minimization and denial of physical violence, economic exploitation, social isolation, verbal abuse, threats and intimidation, physical violence, sexual assault, and captivity. The systematic violence emphasizes the victim's worthlessness except in her role as prostitute.

A Continuum of Violence

Clearly, violence is the norm for women in prostitution. Incest, sexual harassment, verbal abuse, stalking, rape, battering and torture are points on a continuum of violence, all of which occur regularly in prostitution. A difference between prostitution and other types of gender violence is the payment of money for the abuse. Yet payment of money does not erase all that we know about sexual harassment, rape and domestic violence.

The experiences of a woman who prostituted primarily in strip clubs, but also in massage, escort and street prostitution, are typical. In strip club prostitution, she was sexually harassed and assaulted. Stripping required her to smilingly accommodate customers' verbal abuse. Customers grabbed and pinched her legs, arms, breasts, buttocks and crotch, sometimes resulting in bruises and scratches. Customers squeezed her breasts until she was in severe pain, and they humiliated her by ejaculating on her face. Customers and pimps physically brutalized her. She was severely bruised from beatings and frequently had black eyes. Pimps pulled her hair as a means of control and torture. She was repeatedly beaten on the head with closed fists, sometimes resulting in unconsciousness. From these beatings, her eardrum was damaged, and her jaw was dislocated and remains so many years later. She was cut with knives. She was burned with cigarettes by customers who smoked while raping her. She was gang-raped and she was also raped individually by at least 20 men at different times in her life. These rapes by johns and pimps sometimes resulted in internal bleeding.

Yet this woman described the psychological damage of prostitution as far worse than the physical violence. She explained that prostitution "is internally damaging. You become in your own mind what these people do and say with you."

Almost two decades earlier, Norwegian researchers noted that women in prostitution were treated like commodities into which men masturbate, causing immense psychological harm to the person acting as receptacle.

Posttraumatic Stress Disorder

Exposure to paid or unpaid sexual violence may result in symptoms of PTSD. Most prostitution includes the traumatic stressors that are categorized as DSM-IV criterion A1 of the diagnosis of PTSD:

> Direct personal experience of an event that involves actual or threatened death or serious injury, or other threat to

Table 1

Clinical Findings Regarding Violence in All Types of Prostitution

• 95% of those in prostitution experienced sexual harassment that would be legally actionable in another job setting.

• 85% – 95% of those in prostitution want to escape it but have no other options for survival.

• 80% – 90% of those in prostitution have experienced verbal abuse and social contempt, which has adversely affected them.

• 75% of those in prostitution have been homeless at some point.

• 70% – 95% were physically assaulted in prostitution.

• 68% of 854 people in several different types of prostitution in nine countries met criteria for PTSD.

• 65% – 95% of those in prostitution were sexually assaulted as children.

• 60% – 70% were raped in prostitution.

SOURCE: M. Farley

one's personal integrity; or witnessing an event that involves death, injury, or a threat to the physical integrity of another person.

In response to these events, the person with PTSD experiences fear and powerlessness, oscillating between emotional numbing and emotional/physiologic hyperarousal. Posttraumatic stress disorder is known to be especially severe when the stressor is planned and implemented (as in war, rape, incest, battering, torture or prostitution).

In nine countries, across widely varying cultures, we found that two-thirds of 854 women in prostitution had symptoms of PTSD at a severity that was comparable to treatment-seeking combat veterans, battered women seeking shelter, rape survivors, and refugees from state-organized torture.

The women were interviewed in a range of contexts. Interviewers from supportive local agencies accompanied the researchers, and agency referrals were given in writing. In some countries, women and girls were interviewed at agencies that offered services specifically to women and girls in prostitution (Colombia, Thailand, Zambia). Elsewhere, women were interviewed in an STD clinic (Germany, Turkey), in the street (Canada, United States), or in brothels, strip clubs and massage parlors, as well as in the street (Mexico, South Africa). Women often reported that they prostituted in both indoor and outdoor locations.

The intensity of trauma-related symptoms was related to the intensity of involvement in prostitution. Women who serviced more customers in prostitution reported more severe physical symptoms. The longer women were in prostitution, the more STDs they were likely to have experienced.

The Danger of Labeling Prostitution Sex Work

It is a cruel lie to suggest that decriminalization or legalization will protect anyone in prostitution. It is not possible to protect someone whose source of income exposes them to the likelihood of being raped on average once a week. One woman explained that prostitution is "like domestic violence taken to the extreme." Another woman said, "What is rape for others, is normal for us."

Much of the literature has viewed prostitution as a vocational choice. Yet the notion that prostitution is work tends to make its harm invisible. Prostitution is institutionalized and mainstreamed when it is considered to be unpleasant but legitimate "sex work." Even organizations such as the World Health Organization and Amnesty International USA have made the policy error of defining prostitution as a job rather than as human rights abuse.

The solutions are complex. Organizations offering assistance to prostitutes must be queried about whether they offer not only condoms and unions, but also options for escape such as housing and job training. It is essential to abolish not only prostitution, but its root causes as well: sex inequality, racism and colonialism, poverty, prostitution tourism, and economic development that destroys traditional ways of living.

Prostitution Is Not a Choice

Despite the illogical attempt of some to distinguish prostitution from trafficking, trafficking is simply the global form of prostitution. Sex trafficking may occur within or across international borders, thus women may be either domestically or internationally trafficked or both. Young women are trafficked—taken and sold for sexual use—from the countryside to the city, from one part of town to another, and across international borders to wherever there are customers.

It is a clinical and a statistical error to assume that most women in prostitution have consented. Instead of the question, "Did she voluntarily consent to prostitution?" the more relevant question would be, "Did she have real alternatives to prostitution for survival?" The incidence of homelessness (75%) among our respondents and their desire to get out of prostitution (89%) reflect their lack of options for escape.

Until it is understood that prostitution and trafficking can appear voluntary but are not really free choices made from a range of options, it will be difficult to garner adequate support to assist those who wish to escape but have no other economic choices. The conditions that make genuine consent possible are absent from prostitution: physical safety, equal power with customers and real alternatives.

Just as clinicians now screen for physical and sexual abuse and substance abuse history, prostitution history should be addressed at intake. It should be re-addressed after a therapeutic relationship is established, since an initial denial of prostitution is not unusual. The questions "Have you ever exchanged sex for money, drugs, housing, food or clothes?" and "Have you ever worked in the sex industry: for example, dancing, escort, massage, prostitution, pornography or phone sex?" are routine in our intake inquiry. We also recommend asking the question, "Have you ever had sex of any kind with a professional sex worker [call girl, escort, massage parlor worker or prostitute]?"

In addition to acute and chronic PTSD, comorbid diagnoses may include generalized anxiety disorder, mood disorders (including depressive and bipolar disorders), acute suicidality, substance abuse and dependence, personality disorders, dissociative disorders, and symptoms of traumatic brain injury. Although special clinics and shelters for women escaping prostitution are recommended, at this time, services are sometimes accessed at rape crisis centers, public health agencies, substance abuse treatment clinics, shelters for battered women and community mental health clinics.

Certainly there is an urgent need to address the mental health needs of women during prostitution and after escape. However, it is equally important to address men's demand for prostitution. Acceptance of prostitution is one of a cluster of harmful attitudes that encourage and justify violence against women. Violent behaviors against women have been associated with attitudes that promote men's beliefs that they are entitled to sexual access to women, that they are superior to women and that they are licensed as sexual aggressors. Customers of prostitutes strongly endorse these attitudes toward women.

Although a statistical minority, the college-aged customers of prostitutes we surveyed were significantly different from the other young men. Those college students who had purchased women in prostitution were more accepting of prostitution myths and rape myths than the other students. Chillingly, the college-aged customers of prostitutes differed from the other students not only in their attitudes but in their actual behaviors toward women. They acknowledged having perpetrated more sexually coercive acts with their partners than the other men in the survey.

Those of us concerned with human rights must address the social invisibility of prostitution, the massive denial regarding its harms, its normalization as an inevitable social evil, and the failure to educate students of psychiatry, psychology and public health. Prostitution and trafficking can only exist in an atmosphere of public, professional and academic indifference.

Periodical Bibliography

The following articles have been selected to supplement the diverse views presented in this chapter.

Christina Ahn	"The Most Complicated Profession," *Women's Health Activist*, November/December 2004.
Charles Colson	"Downplaying Evil: Is Prostitution 'Empowering'?" *Break Point*, August 23, 2005.
Rochelle L. Dalla	"Night Moves: A Qualitative Investigation of Street-Level Sex Work," *Psychology of Women Quarterly*, March 2002.
Jo Doezma	"Who Gets to Choose? Coercion, Consent, and the UN Trafficking Protocol," *Gender & Development*, March 2002.
Michelle French	"Trust Us, Don't Bust Us," *Herizons*, Fall 2003.
Deborah Jones	"Revisiting the Sex Trade," *Time*, May 17, 2004.
Lee Lakeman	"Prostitution Inseparable of Violence Against Women," Sisyphe.org, June 2, 2005. http://sisyphe.org
Irena Maryniak	"The New Slave Trade," *Index on Censorship*, April 2003.
Heather Lee Miller	"Trick Identities: The Nexus of Work and Sex," *Journal of Women's History*, Winter 2004.
Janice G. Raymond	"Sex Trafficking Is Not 'Sex Work,'" *Conscience*, Spring 2005.
Laura Velm	"Think Again on Sex/Not for Sale: Feminists Resisting Prostitution and Pornography," *Social Alternatives*, 2005.
Amelia Wigton	"'Marie Claire' Puts a Positive Spin on Prostitution," *CWA*, July 20, 2005.

OPPOSING
VIEWPOINTS®
SERIES

CHAPTER 3

What Factors Contribute to Prostitution?

Chapter Preface

One of several factors that commentators claim contribute to prostitution and sex trafficking is the fact that many of the world's women live in poverty. According to AVERT, an international AIDS charity, in many developing nations "women's lack of economic power enables their sexual exploitation." The United Nations and human rights organizations such as AVERT have concluded that prostitution and other forms of sexual exploitation are a result of what science writer Bruce Bower calls a "toxic brew of poverty mixed with a lack of education and job training." Anti-prostitution programs conducted by these organizations therefore "focus on promoting better schooling for girls and teaching vocational skills to villagers," claims Bower.

Some analysts contend, however, that the assumed connection between poverty and prostitution leads to broad and simplistic solutions that are inadequate to help women escape prostitution. "If policy makers are serious about ending the problem," argues anthropologist Lisa Rende Taylor of the Asia Foundation, a research and policy organization, "it is important to get away from unhelpful stereotypes." Rende Taylor directed a 14-month study of child labor, prostitution, and sex trafficking in two northern Thai villages. The study found that "neither poverty nor lack of education are the driving forces behind [the sexual] trafficking of northern Thai children." Her research reveals that girls from both poor and relatively well-off rural Thai families become prostitutes. Thai women, Rende Taylor explains, feel obligated to repay their parents for past sacrifices and to improve the family's financial standing. This obligation extends to parents who earn a decent living. Prostitution, claims Rende Taylor, is a "bearable choice" for northern Thai girls. While first-born girls stay at home to help parents, middle-born girls are seen as financial helpers. "It's common for one female sibling to be working in the fields alongside the parents, another to be working [as a prostitute] in a bar in Bangkok, and perhaps another getting a secondary education," maintains Rende Taylor. The problem of prostitution and sex trafficking among women and girls from rural northern Thailand is therefore a result not of poverty but of the cultural requirement that girls earn money to improve the family's financial status, she concludes. Heather Montgomery of the Open University in Milton Keynes, England, confirms these conclusions. A 12-year-old Thai girl who had earned enough money from one sex client to rebuild her parents' house told Montgomery, "I will make merit for looking after my parents." According to Montgomery, this young Buddhist girl believed that the merit she earned in this life would in her next life negate the effect of having been a prostitute.

Many feminists support the idea that cultural factors, not poverty, lead women into prostitution.

According to [the late] militant feminist Andrea Dworkin,

> Poverty alone does not provide a pool of women for men to f--- on demand. Poverty is insufficient to create that pool of women, no matter how hungry women get. So, in different cultures, societies are organized differently to get the same result: not only are women poor, but the only thing of value a woman has is her so-called sexuality, which, along with her body, has been turned into a sellable commodity. Her so-called sexuality becomes the only thing that matters; her body becomes the only thing that anyone wants to buy.

Whether poverty or cultural factors drive a person to a life of prostitution remains a controversial question. In the following chapter authors from across the globe debate what factors they believe contribute to prostitution and sex trafficking.

> *"People who were sexually abused as children are a whopping 27.7 times more likely than others to be arrested for prostitution."*

Childhood Sexual Abuse Often Leads to Prostitution

Kari Lydersen

Many women who become prostitutes have been victims of childhood sexual abuse, argues Kari Lydersen in the following viewpoint. To cope with the trauma of sexual abuse and the stress of prostitution, she claims, many turn to drugs and alcohol, which further complicate their problems. If society is to prevent prostitution, she maintains, it must condemn the sexual abuse of women and children. Lydersen, a freelance journalist, teaches at the Urban Youth International Journalism Program in Chicago.

As you read, consider the following questions:

1. According to Lydersen, by what percentage has the number of incarcerated women grown?

2. Why do many women turn to paid dates, in the author's view?

3. In the author's opinion, how does sexism play a role in the challenges faced by prostitutes?

Kari Lydersen, "Vicious Circle: Shedding Light on a Cycle of Abuse," *In These Times*, November 17, 2003. Reproduced by permission of the publisher, www.inthesetimes.com.

Growing up on Chicago's South Side, Brenda Myers looked up to the prostitutes working outside her window. "I asked my grandmother what those women were doing. She said, 'They take their panties off for money.'"

At age 9 this idea didn't strike Myers as odd—a family member had been molesting her for years—and she grew up understanding that her body would be the way she got by: "I was thinking, well, they're already taking my panties off, and I wasn't getting any money. So I'll make them pay for it," she says.

She did, and like a majority of women working the streets, Myers became mired in a cycle of dependency on drugs, alcohol, prostitution and abusive relationships—a cycle that starts in youth and ends up landing them in jail and prison.

Women are the fastest growing segment of the incarcerated—more than 91,000 were in state and federal prisons in 2000 (a figure that does not include jails). While the number of incarcerated men grew by 77 percent between 1990 and 2000, the female population grew by 108 percent, according to U.S. Department of Justice [DOJ] statistics.

Like Myers, about half the women behind bars are there for nonviolent offenses, primarily prostitution- and drug-related violations and petty theft or fraud, according to the DOJ.

Childhood Experiences Loom Large

And like Myers, a significantly high number of them are victims of childhood sexual abuse. A . . . study by the Chicago Coalition for the Homeless reported that 41 percent of women arrested for prostitution-related offenses in Cook County jail were sexually abused as children.

The Illinois Coalition Against Sexual Assault (ICASA) conducted a study in which 57 percent of women working as prostitutes in the state reported they were sexually abused as children. The study also found that more than 90 percent lost their virginity through assault, and 70 percent believed being sexually abused as children influenced their decision to become prostitutes.

Likewise, a 1995 study by the National Criminal Justice Reference Service found that people who were sexually abused as children are a whopping 27.7 times more likely than others to be arrested for prostitution.

As Myers describes, many prostitutes say they turned to paid dates as a way to take control of their sexuality after having had it taken from them. Others are forced into prostitution by their abusers—a 2001 study by the Center for Impact Research (CIR) noted that it is common for adults in particularly dire circumstances to force children into prostitution to pay rent or to buy drugs.

A number of women interviewed in Chicago tell similar stories of how they ended up in and out of jail on drug- and prostitution-related offenses. It starts with childhood sexual abuse by a relative or mother's boyfriend, a lifelong psychological trauma for which they often never receive counseling or treatment. Growing up in households where substance abuse and prostitution are prevalent, the women started both at a young age. According to the CIR study, 62 percent of prostitutes have their first "date" [a euphemism for meeting with a prostitute] before age 18.

"My mother's ex-husband used to have me up in the middle of the night giving him head," says Louise Lofton, another former prostitute in Chicago, who has worked with Myers to form a group called Exodus to help women leave prostitution.

"One time she came in unexpectedly, and he started beating her because he knew he was in the wrong; he wanted to cover up for himself," Lofton says. "I ran into him once when I was in prostitution—I had this leopard print skirt on. I said, 'This is because of you.' He said, 'I'm sorry.' I said, '[F---] you.'"

The Link Between Prostitution and Sexual Abuse

- 66% of prostitutes were sexually abused from the ages of 3–16. The average age of victimization was 10.

- 66% of prostitutes abused in childhood were molested by natural, step-, or foster fathers. 10% were sexually abused by strangers.

- More than 90% of prostitutes lost their virginity through sexual assault.

- 70% of prostitutes believe that being sexually abused as children influenced their decisions to become prostitutes.

- 91% of prostitutes sexually abused as children told no one. Only 1% received counseling for the effects of the abuse.

Illinois Coalition Against Sexual Assault,
"By the Numbers: Prostitution," 2001.

Untreated Addictions

Studies also show that almost all women working in prostitution use drugs and alcohol heavily. Many start using these substances or increase their usage in order to deal with the stress and emotional issues of the trade. Others begin to prostitute themselves to fund their drug habits or those of their partners or family members.

For many, the specter of sexual abuse lies behind it all—driving them to seek solace or release in drugs and sex and complicating attempts to change their lives and recover.

"The drug abuse is just one part of it," says Tracy Banks-Geiger, the court and jail program coordinator at Genesis House, a free residential recovery program for women in prostitution in Chicago. "There are also issues of poverty, racism and childhood sexual abuse that never received any treatment."

Doing Harder Time

Women bear the brunt of prostitution incarcerations. Johns usually face heavy fines—under a Chicago city ordinance they are charged $700 in fines and car impoundment fees—but then, in the vast majority of cases, charges are dropped. Male pimps are likewise rarely arrested.

Along with this sexism, racism also plays in the challenges and threats faced by prostitutes. ICASA says that while 40 percent of street prostitutes are women of color, women of color constitute 55 percent of those arrested and 85 percent of those sentenced to jail time.

Dealing with sexual abuse and related traumas is key to breaking the cycle of incarceration and abuse. But most prisons and jails offer little in the way of support groups and counseling, and it can be even harder to access free resources once women get out.

Piecing Together a Life

In Chicago, several former prostitutes report that they were finally able to leave the lifestyle after finding support groups and programs that addressed both substance abuse and the physical and psychological issues involved in their early lives. Many women have had success at Genesis House, the only institution in the city accredited by the courts as an alternative to jail time. Genesis House is a strict yearlong residential program available free to walk-ins and women referred by the courts.

"They're very gentle and patient with me and don't rush me into anything," says a 32-year-old Genesis House resident who asked that her name not be used. "They're helping me build up all those things that had been ripped out of me by prostitution."

In general, recovering prostitutes and service providers have a tricky balance to keep. They need to avoid stigmatizing or condemning prostitution as a lifestyle choice and female sexuality as a whole while still acknowledging that, for many, prostitution is a piece of a painful puzzle they want to leave behind.

To break the cycle of sexual abuse, prostitution, drugs and incarceration, many women note that there must be fundamental change in a society that allows or even encourages the exploitation of children and women.

"If it wasn't for men you wouldn't have prostitution," Myers says. "They think it's a joke, she's having a ball. No she isn't! They think they didn't do anything wrong. Women need to be taught that their body isn't an offering or a sacrifice."

> "Danielle [was] doing whatever she had
> to do to support her addiction to crack
> cocaine and heroin: anal, oral, and
> vaginal sex."

Drug Addiction Can Lead to Prostitution

Afefe Tyehimba

*To support their drug addictions, some addicts turn to prostitu-
tion, asserts Afefe Tyehimba in the following viewpoint. To support her claim, Tyehimba relates the story of a woman trying to
escape the grip of addiction and prostitution. Danielle, whose
name has been changed to protect her anonymity, was introduced to drugs by her drug-dealing boyfriend. When he went to
prison, Danielle began dating hustlers, dealing and using drugs
herself. Ultimately, addiction to crack cocaine led her to prostitution, the author maintains. Tyehimba was a staff writer for the
Baltimore, Maryland,* City Paper.

As you read, consider the following questions:

1. In Tyehimba's opinion, why may the reported number of
   women involved in prostitution in Baltimore be too
   high or too low?

2. What did Danielle claim she lacked as a child?

Afefe Tyehimba, "Along Came a Spiral," *City Paper,* March 31, 2004. Reproduced by
permission of the author. Part 2 of this article appeared in *City Paper,* April 7, 2004.

3. What, in Danielle's opinion, is a "functional user"?

In a sunlit office in lower Charles Village [a Baltimore, Maryland, community], a pair of smiling but wary brown eyes rise from a notepad to assess a stranger standing in the doorway. The office belongs to an acquaintance who has arranged the meeting. The eyes belong to a former drug addict named Danielle (whose name has been changed for this article). The visitor is a reporter carrying her own notepad and a head full of personal questions.

Right off, Danielle's glowing skin, healthy frame, and crisp diction don't jibe with images that come to mind when you picture drug addicts in this city—even ones that have been clean a year. Danielle's ladylike mannerisms also differ from typical around-the-way[1] girls: There's the elegant waft of a hand, daintily crossed ankles, back ramrod straight. Look closer, though, and lingering evidence of Danielle's addiction surfaces—the stuffy breaths she takes through a nose that is still regenerating lost cartilage, the way tears tumble down cheeks as soon as Danielle opens up about the drugs—and what they made her do.

Supporting an Addiction

For 10 years, Danielle "spiraled up and down," doing whatever she had to do to support her addiction to crack cocaine and heroin: anal, oral, and vaginal sex; threesomes; spankings and urination games—a laundry list of services she reluctantly rattles off while recounting, during a series of interviews, what led her into prostitution, and her often stymied efforts to try and get out. "I'm willing to do whatever I can to help somebody else or help people understand," the 32-year-old mom says, tears falling and voice cracking. "But it's hard . . . I mean, I know God has forgiven me. I just have to forgive myself."

---

1. An "around-the-way" girl is urban slang for a tough, neighborhood girl, often one who has sex with many boys in the neighborhood.

Drug-free for a year, but released from jail [in September 2003], Danielle faces a long, uphill climb to reclaim her life and make something entirely different of it. During interviews with women's advocates, service providers, social workers, law enforcement and judicial personnel, academicians, health officials, and other people (still) in the life, it became clear that Danielle's success, along with that of other Baltimoreans seeking to recover from prostitution, requires multifaceted treatment and support—everything from drug treatment to job training to housing assistance, family reunification to long-term talk therapy.

A Tall Order

It's a tall order for services that are in short supply—which means that each day Danielle, who is still in a court-ordered drug treatment program, taps into her own reserve, "reaching for my cup of hope.

"I know that [prostitution] could happen to anybody. Just because a person is a worker, they're still a person," she says, voicing what for her, and others in similar shoes, is a tentative—and tenuous—sense of redemption.

There are about 25,000 women involved in prostitution in Baltimore City, according to figures supplied by You Are Never Alone, a local nonprofit group that offers services to about 2,500 women and girls each year. That overall number, which excludes male and transgender sex workers, could be too high or low. There are no tracking systems or reports specifically for prostitution within local or state law-enforcement agencies, and often legal charges against or health treatment provided for prostitutes are attributed to drug use, not their trade. . . .

Charlotte Cooksey, a Baltimore City District Court judge for 20 years and a member of the [Prostitution Task Force], says any effective solutions will require both official and public support—the former because solutions will take funding and dedicated resources, the latter because, while most people abhor prostitution, few really understand the plight of sex workers.

"In most articles, you can't see their faces, their pain, their experiences," Cooksey says. "Without that, people tend to minimize the struggle and find it much easier to put [prostitutes] aside."

For women like Danielle, however, a blind eye is no option.

On a frigid February [2004] day, Danielle sits down to a Chinese buffet lunch in Mount Vernon, glad to have worn a warm sweatsuit. Not just because of the weather, but because "it helps to keep away the looks," she says, referring to unwanted glances from men. "The looks" have also prompted her . . . to stack 40 pounds onto a previously size 7–8 figure, extra weight that makes Danielle physically uncomfortable and wreaks havoc on her vanity.

Recalling the Past

Danielle smiles, though, when recalling her appearance late on the night of May 25, 1990. She'd just graduated from Woodlawn High School, had spent a night out partying with Troy (not his real name), her first boyfriend, and was about to lose her virginity in the playground of a Woodlawn-area elementary school. Troy was a perfect gentleman, spreading a blanket and taking his time. After all, Danielle was the daughter of a church deacon, a good girl who'd held out during their senior-year relationship.

Eighteen at the time, Danielle says she was "in awe—I had never allowed anybody to get that close to me because I valued my body," adding with a husky, Kool-tinged laugh how she and Troy acted "like bunnies" after that first night. In hindsight, Danielle says she'd fallen blindly in love and was naive to the point where, despite warning signs, her formerly "beautiful, really good" life was shattered. "I learned the hard way that you never make a man your whole world," she says.

Danielle grew up in Baltimore County with strict Catholic parents who she says worked hard as a teacher and government worker to give her and her younger brother just about anything they asked for. A good student and total tomboy, Danielle recalls hating the frilly dresses she wore to church and the smell of a hot comb going through her hair. "I played basketball, baseball, and read a lot of books—I always had a Bible when I couldn't find anything else to read," she says. And if the *Mickey Mouse Club* was on television, her parents knew where to find her.

When asked if she lacked anything as a child, all Danielle can come up with is "maybe some more attention." Her parents worked long hours, making her and her brother latchkey kids. "But really, that's not why," she offers, anticipating her questioner's thoughts.

What then?

"I don't know."

Was there some other abuse, maybe? Something from when she was little?

"That's what you hear from a lot of women. But no, that wasn't it."

Why, Danielle?

"I didn't love myself. I had to learn to love myself."

In Love with a Dope Dealer

Back then, it was Troy who had all of Danielle's love. He was "the only guy in high school who wore a fur," she recalls. He showered her with presents, like a two-carat diamond necklace and blinging rings. Troy told Danielle his family owned a jewelry store, which explained why he could afford his own place, a nice car, and whatever expensive trinkets Danielle wanted. She didn't lack for material things—her mom "used to tell Troy don't think he was giving me anything they couldn't

The Prostitution-Drug Trade Connection

Prostitution and the drug trade go hand in hand. Customers for sex often are buyers for drugs also. Many pimps are supporting their own habits, and dealing drugs as well.

The pimps consider drugs and alcohol a cost of doing business. Without the chemicals, their "livestock" may become psychotic or commit suicide. In addition to the brainwashing and violence, addiction provides a form of control. Drugs also produce isolation from people who otherwise might try to protect a victim or help her escape. The only creature less worthy of help than a prostitute, is an addicted prostitute.

Joe Parker, Lola Greene Baldwin Foundation, August 4, 1998.

buy," she says—but Danielle saw the gifts as expressions of his love.

The summer after graduation, after a blowup with her "old school" family about staying out overnight, Danielle moved in with Troy, nixing previous plans to attend Hampton University (her angry parents refused to pay) and enrolling instead at Coppin State College, where she begged for and managed to get an athletic scholarship. A few months into the live-in arrangement, Danielle began to think it strange how Troy always had business that kept him out late at night, and how he never took her to the jewelry store.

One day Danielle came home early from class and discovered drug paraphernalia on the kitchen table, proof that Troy was a dope dealer. Deciding to "lay in the bed I'd made," Danielle stayed with him, asked no questions ("I never saw anything again," she says), and continued to live well for several years—until Troy's cheating made her leave him.

"He did a girl just because she didn't used to pay attention to him before he had money," she recalls.

Knowing she couldn't go back home, Danielle moved in with her grandmother on the city's west side and continued an on-again-off-again relationship with Troy. A year later, though, Troy was busted and sentenced to 20 years in prison.

Dating Hustlers

Danielle was 22. She'd never used drugs and had only slept with one guy. Although she felt hurt and betrayed by Troy, she missed what he'd given her—kindness, stability, fun times, and spoiling. Danielle started dating "hustlers" who'd seen her around with Troy, and who thought themselves equipped to meet her expectations.

"That really started me to being a kept woman," Danielle says, finishing her lunch and fishing for a cigarette that, memories having resurfaced, it looks like she needs.

In hindsight, Danielle calls the relationships she had going on with men at the time a latent form of tricking—"that's really what it was," she says. But the choices she made run similar to options chosen by, and offered to, generations of women. Books on women's studies abound with descriptions of societal roles of women being receivers of men's affections, such affections often being accompanied by gifts like the proverbial flowers and candy. But historically speaking, says Laura McGough, a postdoctoral fellow in sexually transmitted disease prevention at the Johns Hopkins University School of Medicine, there's always been an element of "judgmentalism" around women and sexual behavior, including, of course, prostitution. . . .

Moving Toward Crisis

When Baltimore has become a shadow of its former industrialized self, when the city's poorest neighborhoods remain awash in heroin and crack cocaine, when federal government efforts tend to be geared toward boosting the NASDAQ,[2] not social programs—more and more people like Danielle are finding themselves in a sex- and drug-induced crisis.

It is another cold afternoon, and Danielle is giving a tour of sorts. Near the intersection of North Avenue and Eutaw Place, riding in the passenger seat of a car, Danielle points to houses where she used to take johns (who paid residents a minimal fee for the use of a room). On Reisterstown Road in West Baltimore, she points to a car repair shop where the owner looked forward to her regular visits. "There, there, and there," she says, pointing to rowhouses in Reservoir Hill. Danielle hesitates, but points out litter-filled alleyways and abandoned buildings too. "Sometimes, when you're sick you just don't care," she says.

With Troy locked up and relationships with other men going sour, it wasn't long before Danielle tried to take matters into her own hands and deal drugs herself. "I'd been watching hustlers," she says, explaining her growing skill at sifting and "scrambling" raw heroin with cutting agents like quinine. She used old lottery tickets as wrappers, and says she enjoyed working for herself. Then, just before she turned 23, Danielle committed a dealer's first deadly sin: She used.

"I dumped [some heroin] the size of a pack of Kool-Aid on a table one day, and sniffed half of it," she recalls, adding that, to her surprise, she didn't feel a thing. "I called a friend, laughing, and they told me to smoke a cigarette. I took one puff, vomited, and then it was like, 'Wow.' Everything, every worry, went away."

Several weeks went by in a pleasant haze, then reality checked in on Danielle. "I went to Cherry Hill one day to see a girlfriend," she says, "and I was feeling real sick, like I had the flu but worse. I was sweating, had diarrhea. People were telling me I had a habit, but I was like, 'Nah.'"

---

2. National Association of Securities Dealers Automated Quotation. A U.S. stock price index for companies listed on the NASDAQ exchange.

The girlfriend suggested they try a trip to Mondawmin Mall, to see if she could shake it off. Six hours later, things had gotten decidedly worse. "My shirt was wet, my nose was running, eyes watering—I couldn't take it," Danielle says. "I sat down and took a sniff from my gold case—and everything *instantly* went away." She says she barely heard her friend saying, "See, you're hooked."

Life slowly changed for Danielle. For the next five years she sometimes sold drugs, and sometimes worked legit jobs—anything to make sure she could get her powder and avoid getting sick. Anything also meant sleeping with hustlers who, in turn, gave her drugs or money or both. Danielle says she was a "functional user" who maintained her looks, who didn't feel she was turning tricks or was somehow desperate.

Crack Cocaine

That changed when, in her late 20s, Danielle was introduced to crack cocaine.

She'd been hanging out in one of numerous houses in the city that serve as hangouts for drug users and dealers—places where, Danielle says, "you take $200 or $1,000, and you plan to stay for a whole weekend." Of course, you run through the money faster than that, she says, but you still enjoy the company "of people who accept you and don't worry about if you paid your gas bill. Your heart's beating fast, but for that moment you forget about your problems."

It's hard not to wonder what, besides a drug habit, Danielle's problems were. In hindsight, so does she, crying when mention is made of Troy and missing her lost innocence, crying harder when mention is made of what had become a major separation with her parents, who hardly saw her anymore.

"With crack, the first hit you take is the hit you want again, but you never get it," Danielle says. "With heroin, over a period of time, you *need* it. But crack takes you and you run with it."

Danielle says she recalls going as many as four days without sleep, then sniffing lots of heroin to "get to an even keel—it's a cycle." In two months, Danielle lost 50 pounds, her skin turned ashen and gray, and her breasts "shriveled to prunes." Even worse, friendly houses and generous hustlers had gotten harder to come by.

Then came the man in the Volvo who, after passing her by a couple of times as she walked along North Avenue, flagged Danielle down. They talked. It was time for a fix, but she still felt indignant. She says she asked the man "Do I have a sign that says 'pussy' written on my head?"

They talked some more, and drove off together. For two minutes of oral sex, she got $60 and a ride to a spot where she could cop.

"After you do it once, the second, third, or fourth times don't matter," Danielle says. "Already, [after the first john], I was thinking how much I could make if I got one or two more dates that day. It wasn't about getting high anymore—you can't even call it getting high. It's the fear of getting sick, that's what keeps you out there. Every day you wake up, hoping you got at least $10 to get out the gate."

| "*Globalisation and gender prejudice in patriarchy make the girl child fall as the first victim in every vulnerable family.*"

Poverty and Gender Inequality Promote Prostitution

Joy Aghatise Evbuomwan

Poverty increases the plight of women who already suffer from gender inequality, asserts Joy Aghatise Evbuomwan in the following viewpoint. Evbuomwan, a Nigerian activist and program director of the Gender and Governance division of the African Network for Environmental and Economic Justice, argues that many women and young girls have no choice but to become prostitutes. When families are too poor to make ends meet, she contends, girls are often forced to trade sex for much-needed money. Rather than punish young girls who have become prostitutes, nations worldwide should eliminate the root causes of prostitution: poverty and gender inequality, she maintains.

As you read, consider the following questions:

1. According to Evbuomwan, what percentage of the world's 1.3 billion absolute poor are women?

Joy Aghatise Evbuomwan, "Poverty, Prostitution, and the Girl Child," *ECONDAD*. Reproduced by permission.

2. Why are women disproportionately affected in the aftermath of caste wars, political strife, and domestic conflicts, in the author's view?

3. In the author's opinion, what often happens to female graduates struggling to get jobs in some countries?

Extreme poverty and [a] falling standard of living have increasingly dogged the Nigerian state. An average Nigerian is hungry, poor and seriously deprived of the basic essentials of livelihood. A walk through any major street in Nigeria reveals that everywhere reeks of poverty. It can be seen on the faces of people daily thronging the streets.

[The] international development community used to think that if a country could sustain rapid growth, poverty would take care of itself. Then it realized that growth does not always translate into poverty reduction, so it started emphasizing "pro-poor" growth. Growth generates more income. But the poor are unlikely to receive a fair share of this increased income if they are not empowered—first economically but also, just as important, socially and politically. The federal and state governments agreed to eradicate poverty but they cannot explain why the resources are not getting to the poor.

Women comprise 70% of the world's 1.3 billion absolute poor. They bear the brunt of economic and financial transition and crisis caused by market forces and globalisation. Within every unit, that of family, community, and sect, the weakest and the most vulnerable are women and girl children due to their life long depravation in education, protection, shelter, skill learning and development, access to resources and rights.

Imbalances in Power

Poverty does not create imbalances in gender and sex. It only aggravates already existing imbalances in power and therefore increases the vulnerability of those who are at the receiving end of gender prejudice. In a patriarchal set up, the section [within] families in societies that is affected is women and girl children. Caste wars, political strife, domestic conflicts through their manifestations and repercussions reflect strong gender prejudice against women. Violence against women, assault and rape on women are not individual sexual or physical crimes. It has become a tool of, a political statement for, aggression and gender persecution, which amply reflects on the degree of human degradation and commodification of women in the eyes of the state, community and society.

Thus globalisation and gender prejudice in patriarchy make the girl child fall as the first victim in every vulnerable family.

At the end of trans-national and intra-national organised networks that control and execute [human] trafficking lies an institution called Prostitution. The increasing demand for younger women and younger children for purposes of prostitution comes through this institution and that is what is sustaining and protecting the network that supplies the desired gender and age through trafficking. The violence of displacement and sale of women and children thus culminates into the violence called Prostitution.

It is very easy to flip through newspapers, radio and television stations and see or hear people pointing accusing fingers at girls for prostituting, condemning the trade, especially international prostitution, and making moves to repatriate them from abroad. But they fail to look beyond these girls and examine the underlining factors that made them go into sex trade.

The Push and Pull Factors

If one were to understand the institution of prostitution, and the process of trafficking that is inextricable to the institution, it may be done through the push and pull factors. The push

Creating a Market for Women's Bodies

Prostitution is one of the most obvious and manifest ways in which women are exploited by men due to the unequal relations created by differences in race, class, gender and nationality. In analyzing the sex industry, therefore, one must begin by analyzing all of the factors that create a market for women's bodies to be sold. Theorists and activists alike strive for answers to the issue of prostitution as an exploitative system where women's rights go unprotected, yet the discourse often only takes into consideration economic factors, not the social, political, or systematic forces creating this market.

Susan Ozawa, Coalition Against Trafficking in Women, 2003.

factors that help to aggravate trafficking of women and children are:

- Poverty
- Discrimination [against] the girl child—rights to health, education, and therefore options, property and resources
- Organized crime rackets
- Debt burden of the family
- Economic disparities in the country
- Migration
- Religious and social sanctions promoting child marriage
- Cultural practices
- Tradition and religion that promotes and supports

prostitution, particularly of the girl child

- Growth of trans-national crime
- Involvement of state agencies that are responsible to check trafficking
- Socialization of violence against women
- Lack of a support structure that would help in combating the demand for women and children for prostitution

Let us consider a man for instance who [has] no means of livelihood but [goes] ahead to raise a large family. He brings children into the world that he cannot take care of. These children grow up to become rogues, delinquents and women of easy virtue when they are barely out of their diapers. Now if these children become adults and get caught in the act, [who] should bear the capital punishment? They or their parents who gave them no choice other than to live the hard way?

The unsavory scourge of prostitution should be dealt with first at home before looking outside. There is this popular saying that one [has] to remove the log in his eyes so that he can see clearly to remove the [mote] in another person's eyes.

What about fresh female graduates who go about struggling to get jobs only for them to be told that they have to go to bed with the directors of such companies before they could secure appointments. Some others get jobs with these new generation banks only to be told that they have to employ their "bodies for Marketing" in order to win rich clients/customers. What do we call that if not prostitution? Prostitution means the use of one's body for sexual activities for the purpose of remuneration or any other form of consideration. Government officials and politicians are not left out. They visit our university campuses at night to recruit female students for the entertainment of visiting senators/top government officials.

Commercial sexual exploitation is illegal and we have to work towards the safe keeping of our children.

What Needs to Be Done?

- Educate all female children

- Stop all forms of discrimination against women/girl children

- Stop most cultural practices that are an affront to the right of women generally, e.g. child marriage, female genital cutting

- Create more programmes that are aimed at eradicating poverty completely from our society

- Give exemplary punishment to traffickers

- Demand and press for the rescue [of] all children forced into prostitution

- Organise strict border security

- Make trafficking and child sexual abuse [a] non-bailable offence

- Provide more income generation programmes for rural poor

A Victim Speaks

This is what a victim of sexual abuse has to say:

"I was poor but happy in my family when my father had to take a second wife. Isn't polygamy bad? My mother was insecure; she fought with my father every day and thus my father deserted us totally.

"I was fourteen and was offered a job in the city. My relative who took me sold me into prostitution. I was forced and sexually abused till I agreed to prostitution. I was sick; I went through six abortions in one year. I was rescued by police in a raid and my madam did not pay for my release. Maybe she knew I had been infected with HIV virus.

"Today I am back home in Nigeria and living in a home. I look healthy, beautiful. I am studying now—I can cook, sew and do other domestic chores but I was told that I shall die soon. But why? I did not ask for it. I had to go from one corner of the world to another because I had no option— was that my fault? Why didn't this society offer me an option? Why?"

Does anyone have an answer?

| "In a bid to escape poverty, terrorism, war and abuse... an increasing number of women are turning to prostitution."

War and Terrorism Increase Prostitution

Kamala Sarup

In the following viewpoint Kamala Sarup, a native of India, claims that women in war-torn nations have limited access to economic resources and few marketable skills. To survive, she argues, poorly educated women in countries torn by war and terrorism often turn to prostitution. Displaced women who have become prostitutes expose themselves to health risks, including HIV/AIDS, Sarup maintains. However, taboos against prostitution prevent governments from distributing condoms or educating women about how to protect themselves, she asserts. Sarup is editor of peacejournalism.com, which promotes peaceful solutions to societies in crisis.

As you read, consider the following questions:

1. In what nations have national authorities failed to halt the abuse of women, according to an Amnesty International report?

Kamala Sarup, "Terrorism and War Increases Prostitution," *Peace Journalism*, July 22, 2005. Reproduced by permission of the author.

2. What options do rural girls in war-torn countries have, in Sarup's view?

3. What alternative income generation strategies does the author recommend?

"Women and girls in war zones suffer rape and violent abuse while offenders escape punishment, because national authorities have failed to act to halt such abuses. Despite promises, treaties and legal mechanisms, governments failed to protect women and girls in conflicts in Colombia, Iraq, Sudan, Chechnya, Nepal and Afghanistan" [an] Amnesty International [report] said.

Amnesty's secretary general, Irene Khan, said in an interview, "What we have seen consistently is that if you don't prosecute and punish, then there is a tendency for [the abuse] to continue. Women and girls are not just killed, they are raped, sexually attacked, mutilated and humiliated." She further said no official statistics were kept, so it was impossible to say whether the situation was worsening.

The report urged political leaders to openly condemn violence against women and cooperate with the court in bringing offenders to justice. It also recommended the urgent provision of medical and humanitarian support for female survivors of abuse.

A Way to Survive in the Streets

Millions of women are involved in prostitution for survival on the streets. Many women see . . . prostitution as a way to freedom from war and terrorism. So, women see in prostitution a way to earn more money.

The prostitution is the direct consequence of economic crisis and the low status afforded to women in the country. Because women have a limited access to occupations and resources, they are the ones hardest hit during [an] economic crisis. Poverty is definitely linked to prostitution. On the other side, it exacerbates an already desperate situation caused by war. Poverty is leading many women into street prostitution.

Today's girls, especially . . . those being raised in the country's conflict-ridden and terrorism-affected rural areas, for the displaced, especially poorly educated teenage girls whose wage-earning skills are often limited [to] working in the fields, there are few options: remain and risk being killed [or] a life of prostitution. War, terrorism and poverty are bringing more and more girls from villages into cities.

Terrorism and war-affected women are also sexually abused. It is important to know if women and girls are turning to prostitution for food and shelter.

In a bid to escape poverty, terrorism, war and abuse in the country, an increasing number of women are turning to prostitution. Prostitutes [are] operating in bars, restaurants and hotels. Some night club owners reportedly allow under-age girls into clubs for sexual exploitation by clients. Most of the displaced are from rural areas and entering urban settings. The search for jobs is complicated. So many girls start having sexual relations, and become prostitutes. . . . The vast majority of women who find themselves as prostitutes are there unwillingly.

Displacement and Prostitution

There have been no studies linking displacement and prostitution. Clearly, reliable studies and data on sexual exploitation and prostitution and the link to displacement are urgently needed.

Unfortunately, one of the only wage-earning options available to many young, poorly educated females is prostitution. The direct impacts of . . . war and terrorism on women are wide ranging. On the other hand, left with no home, no income, women end up begging or prostituting themselves in order to provide food. Terrorism, hunger and war form the

Weapons of War

Among the most severe problems which all children and women face during armed conflicts is a heightened risk of rape, sexual humiliation, prostitution and other forms of gender-based violence. Women of all ages are targets, but adolescent girls are often especially vulnerable since they may be thought less likely to have sexually transmitted diseases, such as HIV/AIDS. While most victims have been girls, young boys are also raped or forced into prostitution—although such cases are generally underreported. These crimes might be seen simply as a consequence of general societal breakdown during wartime, but rape and other forms of gender-based violence are often used systematically as weapons of war. Yet such violence is rarely taken as seriously as it should be.

Graca Machel, Echoes, *2001.*

backdrop to this furtive exchange, for deepening poverty is driving increasing numbers of women to sell their bodies.

Yes, poverty was the main obstacle to the full realization of women's equality. It manifested itself in poor health, low levels of education, food insecurity and unemployment. Further, women constituted the majority of the population living in rural areas, and they suffered the consequences of unsophisticated farming practices and inadequate power infrastructure.

As girls usually have few marketable skills, sex becomes the only avenue for survival. One of the most tragic consequences of . . . terrorism and war has been [the] kidnapping of women and children. Displacement is the most common consequence of war and terrorism and women the most affected population.

In flight as well as upon arrival in big cities, women commonly experience violence and abuse because war and terrorism have contributed to a rise in prostitution, which threatens women's health. In the streets, the girls are under the threat of disease. Prostitution is officially illegal and HIV is widespread among prostitutes in the world. . . . The continuing war and terrorism [have] exacerbated the problem.

Even a cursory look at the situation on the streets indicates that there are many more women and teenagers involved in prostitution than the official statistics suggest. And because some of the countries are a closed society, prostitution is not widely discussed in public. Most of them work as prostitutes, usually for between 10 and 20 dollars. Prostitution appears to be . . . everywhere in the society. Family problems, not unrelated to poverty, may also lead the girls to prostitute themselves.

A Government Failure

Only the women who sold sex faced legal penalties, not the men who bought it. The law continued to hold prostitutes, not their customers, [accountable]. Governments do not distribute condoms. Similarly, reports from the field indicate that large stocks of condoms expire because they go unused. Awareness of the disease and methods of prevention are extremely low in many countries.

However, governments have failed to systematically identify and meet the distinct needs of a large and particularly at-risk [group of] women and have no program for them. Most women made the dangerous choice to sell sex because of financial difficulties and limited opportunities. The number of girls engaged in prostitution has risen. Though there [is] no reliable information, prostitution seems to be a growing phenomenon.

The government does not give licenses to them or require them to be tested regularly. Terrorism, war and political instability in several countries [is responsible] for the unabated prostitution of women.

Inadequate social safety nets have left many women with no choice but to sell their bodies. In addition, poverty brought about by war and terrorism leads to increased prostitution, and . . . few have access to information about how to protect themselves from HIV/AIDS.

When the social infrastructure collapses as a result of terrorism and war, famine, and economic crisis, women turn to prostitution as a last resort. No matter how women and girls get into prostitution, it is difficult to get out. Often women can leave prostitution only after they become ill.

In some cases, it is the parents who sell their girls to foreign paedophiles via local intermediaries. How long will we allow the current situation to continue?

Tackling the Problem

Special attention must be given to the encouragement of economic growth in the rural areas.

For this reason, alternative income generation strategies are needed. A reintegration strategy should include greater training, credit and enterprise opportunities. Those affected most negatively by war and terrorism are women living in poverty, . . . particularly in rural areas; the negative impacts on basic human needs, development and reconstruction must be addressed.

In the name of protecting prostitutes, . . . many NGOs [nongovernmental organizations] are introducing legislation but such legislation does not provide protection. Prostitutes are forced [into the practice] by poverty, violence, terrorism and war.

Women and girls should then be offered protection through programs which tackle the root causes of the problem, lack of security and income. In order to change these things, the economy has to be improved.

> *"By making visas so prohibitively diffi-*
> *cult, Western governments ensure that*
> *Ukrainians, along with migrants from*
> *most of the rest of the world, must turn*
> *to people-smugglers or traffickers."*

Strict Immigration Policies Promote Sex Trafficking

Lily Hyde

Lily Hyde claims in the following viewpoint that the strict immi-
gration policies of rich nations promote sex trafficking. According
to Hyde, these nations rely upon the work performed by illegal
immigrants, but they refuse to offer them legal entry. As a result,
migrants, especially women from impoverished countries such as
Ukraine, use unscrupulous traffickers to help them enter rich
countries so that they can find work. Unfortunately, Hyde main-
tains, many become prostitutes in order to pay off debts to traf-
fickers. Hyde is a freelance journalist in Ukraine.

As you read, consider the following questions:

1. According to Hyde, what are the two faces of trafficking in human beings in Ukraine?

2. In the author's view, why is the sex trade the most visible side of human trafficking?

Lily Hyde, "Green Light, Red Light," *New Internationalist,* December 2004. Copyright © 2004 *New International Magazine.* Reproduced by permission.

3. What must nongovernmental organizations now show to get United Nations support, in the author's opinion?

The advertisement for cash transfers shows a smiling woman cleaning an expensive house. The picture next to her shows a young boy with a new CD player. The caption reads: 'She is transferring something more valuable than money.'

By contrast, the leaflet against [human] trafficking features a shadowy man holding a handful of dollars and a cage with a young woman inside. The caption reads: 'Do you want to exchange your dignity, freedom and health for life in a cage?'

The Problem of Defining Trafficking

These are the two faces of trafficking in human beings in Ukraine—opportunity and menace. One implies that working abroad allows women to provide their children with much more than expensive toys. The other warns that the only work awaiting women who emigrate is slavery and prostitution. Both messages reappear over and over again in the media, in advertising, in popular culture. Even governments use them. But which is the true picture?

Trafficking of people does not just mean transport; it also implies ownership. The UN [United Nations] defines trafficking as 'the recruitment, transportation, transfer, harbouring or receipt of persons, by means of the threat or use of force or other forms of coercion . . . for the purpose of exploitation. Exploitation shall include, at a minimum, the exploitation of prostitution or other forms of sexual exploitation, forced labour or services, slavery or practices similar to slavery, servitude or the removal of organs.'

Trafficking is not the same as people-smuggling, although it is difficult to separate the two. 'The mere facilitation of illegal entry into or through a country is not, on its own, trafficking in persons, although such migrant-smuggling may be part of a trafficking operation or turn into a trafficking situation.'

In countries like Ukraine and Moldova many people are not aware of the finer distinctions. A combination of trafficking and people-smuggling affects an enormous percentage of the working population; in Moldova an estimated third of the workforce is working illegally abroad. In countries like Britain or Italy it's highly likely that illegal and trafficked labour has picked the vegetables you eat or is looking after your old sick grandmother. And East European women have come to dominate the most sensational and troubling aspect of trafficking—prostitution.

Peddling Stereotypes

Despite its illegal or underground status in most countries, the sex trade is the most visible side of human trafficking. It grabs the headlines and has become a journalistic obsession. It still seems to be impossible to talk about sex without getting moralistic. By extension, the trafficked women—the 'Natashas', as all east European sex workers and, by implication, all east European women abroad have come to be called—are easily categorized as helpless victims. They have either been duped into sex work, or else are knowing prostitutes.

Unfortunately it isn't just the media peddling these stereotypes. Governments too confuse trafficking and prostitution in their visa regimes, their policy papers and their anti-trafficking declarations.

One Ukrainian young woman I know—who really is called Natasha—when applying for an Italian visa was told she must first bring a declaration from the police stating that she had never engaged in prostitution. Any legitimate travel agency in Kiev will tell you how hard it is now for a young single Ukrainian woman to get a tourist visa to any West European country.

In 1992 the US State Department report Trafficking in Persons (TIP) was criticized for letting wealthy countries off the hook. But the biggest furore was over morals. A subsequent critical review of the report ignored the labour aspect of trafficking entirely, choosing instead to treat it as simply a matter of prostitution. Indeed, it conflated the two. According to one US advisor: '[Trafficking] is inherently evil and we need to abolish it. That's the approach that we want to take—that this whole commercial sex industry is a human rights abuse.' The review went on to accuse a number of individuals and organizations supported with US Government funds of promoting prostitution and its legalization.

A Moral Minefield

A 2004 report by USAID [United States Agency for International Development], Trafficking in Persons, includes the proviso: 'Organizations advocating prostitution as an employment choice or which advocate or support the legalization of prostitution are not appropriate partners for anti-trafficking grants or contracts.' This has moved a long way from the UN's original definition of trafficking. Anti-trafficking measures, which are aimed at protecting people from violence and exploitation in any labour sphere, have become enmeshed in the moral minefield of whether sex work is a valid form of employment and should be legalized.

Non-governmental organizations (NGOs) now have to show they offer help only to those who are classified as 'victims' and did not know they would be involved in prostitution. NGOs try not to make that distinction. But Winrock International—an American NGO which runs a USAID-funded anti-trafficking project in Ukraine (in partnership with the International Organization for Migration [IOM])—asks any returned woman who appeals to the organization: 'Were you aware you would be involved in the sex industry?'

'We are not helping prostitutes, we are helping the victims of trafficking,' says Oksana Horbunova, from IOM Ukraine. 'That means any person who was kept by an owner without money and forced into labour; it doesn't matter whether it's sex work or in agriculture or the domestic sector.'

Of the 1,386 victims of trafficking that IOM has assisted since 2002 only three are known to be working in the Ukrainian sex industry. The vast majority are now employed by the state or private business. However, I personally know three women sex workers in Ukraine who have been trafficked abroad in quite brutal circumstances. So I can't help but wonder if many trafficked women never approach IOM or other agencies because they fear being classified as prostitutes.

Olga from Nikolaiv, south Ukraine, has been trafficked twice. The first time, in Germany, she honestly thought she'd be dancing in a bar. The second time, in Greece, she knew she'd be doing sex work. She was kept locked in a room with no pay and not even enough food. She doesn't usually talk about the Greece trip because she knows that if a woman is aware of the work she'll be doing she is automatically disqualified from sympathy and 'victim' status.

Promoting Deterrence?

Winrock International's main aim is not to support the women who return but to prevent them from going in the first place—to discourage them from finding jobs abroad in any sector, not just the sex industry. Winrock provides vocational training for women in Ukraine to help them find employment at home. According to their own research, 20,000 women said that the training persuaded them not to seek work abroad, but just 5,000 of those found a job and 400 set up their own businesses.

Anti-trafficking programmes have also made films depicting the horrific situation and shown them in schools to warn young women of the dangers. One NGO staff member told

© Joseph Shoopack.

Josheph Shoopack. © Joseph Shoopack. Reproduced by permission.

me that at one school a girl ran out of the class crying. Her mother was working abroad. After seeing the film, the girl was convinced her mother was a prostitute and in great danger.

Inna Shvab of the NGO La Strada Ukraine disapproves of this policy of deterrence. 'I think it's not entirely correct, because you can't deny someone the chance for a better life. It may be their opportunity; it isn't always bad abroad and we can't offer them any alternatives in Ukraine.'

The Impact of Strict Immigration Policies

The governments funding these programmes are the same ones receiving illegal migrants. By making visas so prohibitively difficult, Western governments ensure that Ukrainians, along with migrants from most of the rest of the world, must turn to people-smugglers or traffickers. Everyone knows that work is available and potentially profitable.

'As long as there is a demand, Ukrainian women will always go because they can be paid more than here,' says Tetyana Rudenko, Crisis Prevention Programme Co-ordinator at Winrock. Some governments admit as much. At a conference in Kiev organized by the Catholic NGO Caritas, a representative from the Interior Ministry in Italy stated that the care system for the elderly there is now entirely propped up by Ukrainian women. Yet Italy is a staunch anti-trafficking ally of the US TIP report criteria. The contradiction is glaring. One of the top destination countries for smuggled and trafficked Ukrainians recognizes that its care system would collapse without them—but it will allow no legal possibilities for Ukrainians to work there.

While shirking any responsibility, these same governments pour money into programmes explaining the horrors of trafficking. Stay at home, is the message—and don't expect too much.

Tania didn't want to listen to that advice. Trafficked to Turkey by a boyfriend, she later set herself up as an independent sex worker but lost most of the profits to thieves. When I met her on the highway outside Nikolaiv, where sex workers line the roadside, she was trying to organize a second trip to Italy.

Tania knew she would have to get into debt to a trafficker who would pay her transport and set her up in work. She wasn't deterred. 'Working for $30 a month here is no way out; I've got to pay for my flat, and my son's schooling. It's up to me to do something. I'm not going to give in to this life, and I'm not doing anything criminal. I'm not risking anything but myself.'

IOM staff, who see the terrified, browbeaten women returning from nightmares abroad, would probably say that risk is too high. Tania died in Ukraine just a few months after I spoke to her. Many of the women I've met over the years working the streets of Ukraine have also died here. The advice to stay at home rings hollow.

Unanswered Questions

'Why can't we go abroad as tourists? Why can't we go and do legal work?' Olena asks. She is from a dead-end town in Moldova and ran away as a teenager, emulating the girls she saw returning with fur coats and gold jewellery. Deported from Turkey, she took off again for the Balkans. This time she came back with nightmares about the abuse and murder of Moldovan women. Were it not for her baby, born soon after her return, and the help of a local NGO, she'd probably have gone abroad again. There are simply no opportunities at home. 'This selling of us girls—I can't understand why it works out like this. Why do our girls have to suffer?'

It's a question that the anti-trafficking films and the government reports never get around to answering. The US TIP report recommends low-cost trafficking deterrents ('Listening to Exploited Children', 'Rewarding Law Enforcement') while not once mentioning how immigration policy might influence the situation. An anti-trafficking leaflet counters the 'myth' that 'working abroad, though illegally, will enable me to see the world . . . ' with the 'reality' that 'travelling as a tourist is a splendid way to do this too. As an illegal migrant your chances of being exploited are greater. . . .' The idea that a girl like

Olena could ever get to visit the West as a tourist is as much of a myth as any of those the anti-traffickers seek to debunk.

Ukrainian women are betrayed just as much by the anti-trafficking poster as by the cash-transfer ad. Until rich countries change their immigration policies, the 'necessary evil' of people-smuggling will continue, with trafficking its uglier underside. And as long as the moralistic stereotypes of 'victim' and 'prostitute' endure, women like Olena, Tania and Olga will be condemned for trying to take their fate into their own hands.

Periodical Bibliography

The following articles have been selected to supplement the diverse views presented in this chapter.

Brian Bergman	"Lost, Luckless Girls," *Maclean's*, May 23, 2005.
Bruce Bower	"Childhood's End," *Science News*, September 24, 2005.
Maddy Coy	"Leaving Care; Loathing Self," *Community Care*, February 3, 2005.
Economist	"It's a Foreigner's Game," September 2, 2004.
Barbara Gunnell	"Nothing to Sell but Their Bodies," *New Statesman*, March 1, 2004.
Harper's	"I Am Going to Burn," March 2004.
Angie Heal	"The Sex Trap," *Community Care*, June 10, 2004.
Dan Luzadder	"Sex Tourism: Propriety, Profits and Exploitation Collide," *Travel Weekly*, July 26, 2004.
Sarah E. Mendelson	"Barracks and Brothels: Peacekeepers and Human Trafficking in the Balkans," *CSIS Report*, February 2005.
Juno Parreñas	"Silence Is Deadly," *Lesbian News*, May 2004.
Corey Rennell	"Saving the Youngest Workers," *Harvard International Review*, Fall 2004.
Philip Yancy	"Back from the Brothel," *Christianity Today*, January 2005.

OPPOSING
VIEWPOINTS®
SERIES

CHAPTER 4

What Policies Should Govern Prostitution?

Chapter Preface

Traditionally, efforts to control prostitution have targeted prostitutes, not their customers. Recently, however, hoping to reduce the demand for prostitution, some communities in North America and Europe have implemented programs that target prostitutes' clients, commonly referred to as "johns." One program offers first-time offenders the opportunity to attend "john school" as an alternative to prosecution. The goal of the program is to discourage johns from visiting prostitutes. At a one-day program in Winnipeg, Manitoba, for example, johns listen to blunt and graphic presentations by attorneys, vice cops, public health officials, former prostitutes, and the angry residents of neighborhoods where the sex trade is epidemic. The use of john schools to reduce the demand for prostitution, like other issues in the debate over what policies should govern prostitution, is controversial. While some claim that the program reduces recidivism, others argue that the program is ineffective, unfair, and dangerous for prostitutes.

Some commentators contend that john schools successfully educate johns about the risks of visiting prostitutes and, as a result, reduce recidivism. According to the district attorney's office in Brooklyn, New York, since the launch of the city's john school in 2002, only two participants have been rearrested. Judy Taylor, a parole supervisor with the Salvation Army in Winnipeg, reports similar success. Of the 350 men who have gone through the Winnipeg program since 1997, only four were rearrested on similar charges. "At first, there's a lot of denial, justification, even anger at being there," claims Taylor. "By the end of the day," she asserts, "some of the same men are in tears. . . . I'm not naïve enough to think that everyone will change their ways. But many do." Some johns credit the school with opening their eyes to the harm their behavior causes. According to one john school participant, "I heard from parents who had built huge fences to keep their kids safe from the creeps who drove around the streets looking for girls." He adds, "I was one of those creeps."

John school critics dispute such claims. J. Marlowe of the Sex Workers Alliance of Vancouver argues that the success of john schools is unproven. "There is no real evidence that the program has [a]ffected recidivism rates," argues Marlowe. Low arrest rates, critics argue, only mean that john school participants are not getting caught again. "What are the odds of someone being arrested more than once for accepting a proposition from a police officer posing as a prostitute?" asks Marlowe. Sex workers and their advocates also contend that having johns go to school while prostitutes must pay stiff fines and spend time in jail is unfair. "John 'schools' provide a way for men to buy their way out of a criminal conviction," maintains Marlowe. "Providing a one-day 'schooling' alternative for johns, while continuing to hand out harsher sentences for women working the street," says Marlowe, "[is] a mockery of justice, and . . . discriminate[s] on the basis of sex." John school opponents also maintain that these programs simply add to the problems prostitutes face. According to Marlowe, "John 'schools' tend to spook the nice guys but not the creeps. . . . Losing these clients means that sex workers have to find new clients, many of whom may not be as pleasant or respectful."

Analysts continue to debate whether john schools are an effective way to reduce the demand for prostitution. The authors in the following chapter debate the impact of several other attempts to reduce prostitution and its accompanying dangers.

*"Legalization of prostitution sends the
message to new generations of men and
boys that women are sexual commodities and that prostitution is harmless
fun."*

Prostitution Should Not Be Legalized

Janice G. Raymond

*In the following viewpoint Janice G. Raymond lists the reasons
why she believes that prostitution should not be legalized. Legalization does not dignify prostitution, she argues; it dignifies the
degradation of women. Moreover, Raymond asserts, legalization
will not improve women's health or protect women from violence
at the hands of pimps and johns. Indeed, she maintains, legalization promotes sex trafficking, increases child prostitution, and
further exploits women whose circumstances force them into a
life of prostitution. Raymond, professor of women's studies and
medical ethics at the University of Massachusetts, is co-executive
director of the Coalition Against Trafficking in Women.*

As you read, consider the following questions:

1. In Raymond's view, why is it important to advocate for
   the decriminalization of prostitutes?

2. According to the author, by what percentage has the sex industry increased in the Netherlands since it legalized prostitution?

3. In the author's opinion, why does it make no sense to mandate health examinations for prostitutes and not customers?

What does legalization of prostitution or decriminalization of the sex industry mean? In the Netherlands, legalization amounts to sanctioning all aspects of the sex industry: the women themselves, the buyers, and the pimps who, under the regime of legalization, are transformed into third party businessmen and legitimate sexual entrepreneurs. Legalization/decriminalization of the sex industry also converts brothels, sex clubs, massage parlors and other sites of prostitution activities into legitimate venues where commercial sexual acts are allowed to flourish legally with few restraints.

Dignifying the Sex Industry

Some people believe that, in calling for legalization or decriminalization of prostitution, they dignify and professionalize the women in prostitution. But dignifying prostitution as work doesn't dignify the women, it simply dignifies the sex industry. People often don't realize that decriminalization means decriminalization of the whole sex industry, not just the women in it. And they haven't thought through the consequences of legalizing pimps as legitimate sex entrepreneurs or third party businessmen, or the fact that men who buy women for sexual activity are now accepted as legitimate consumers of sex.

In countries where women are criminalized for prostitution activities, it is crucial to advocate for the *decriminalization of the women* in prostitution. No woman should be punished for her own exploitation. But States should never decriminalize pimps, buyers, procurers, brothels or other sex establishments.

Promoting Sex Trafficking

Legalized or decriminalized prostitution industries are one of the root causes of sex trafficking. One argument for legalizing prostitution in the Netherlands was that legalization would help to end the exploitation of desperate immigrant women who had been trafficked there for prostitution. However, one report found that 80% of women in the brothels of the Netherlands were trafficked from other countries. In 1994, the International Organization of Migration (IOM) stated that in the Netherlands alone, "nearly 70% of trafficked women were from CEEC [Central and Eastern European Countries]."

The government of the Netherlands presents itself as a champion of anti-trafficking policies and programs, yet it has removed every legal impediment to pimping, procuring and brothels. In the year 2000, the Dutch Ministry of Justice argued in favor of a legal quota of foreign "sex workers," because the Dutch prostitution market demanded a variety of "bodies." Also in 2000, the Dutch government sought and received a judgment from the European Court recognizing prostitution as an economic activity, thereby enabling women from the European Union and former Soviet bloc countries to obtain working permits as "sex workers" in the Dutch sex industry if they could prove that they are self employed. Nongovernmental organizations (NGOs) in Europe report that traffickers use the work permits to bring foreign women into the Dutch prostitution industry, masking the fact that women have been trafficked, by coaching them to describe themselves as independent "migrant sex workers."

In the year since lifting the ban on brothels in the Netherlands, eight Dutch victim support organizations reported an increase in the number of victims of trafficking, and twelve victim support organizations reported that the number of victims from other countries has not diminished. Forty-three of the 348 municipalities (12%) in the Netherlands choose to follow a no-brothel policy, but the Minister of Justice has indicated that the complete banning of prostitution within any municipality could conflict with the federally guaranteed "right to free choice of work."....

Expanding the Sex Industry

Contrary to claims that legalization and decriminalization would control the expansion of the sex industry, prostitution now accounts for 5% of the Netherlands economy. Over the last decade, as pimping was legalized, and brothels decriminalized in the year 2000, the sex industry increased by 25% in the Netherlands. At any hour of the day, women of all ages and races, dressed in hardly anything, are put on display in the notorious windows of Dutch brothels and sex clubs and offered for sale. Most of them are women from other countries who were probably trafficked into the Netherlands....

Australia's Experience

Legalization of prostitution in the State of Victoria, Australia, resulted in massive expansion of the sex industry. Along with legalization of prostitution, other forms of sexual exploitation, such as tabletop dancing, bondage and discipline centers, peep shows, phone sex, and pornography, have all developed in much more profitable ways than before legalization. Prostitution has become an integral part of the tourism and casino boom in Victoria with government-sponsored casinos authorizing the redeeming of casino chips at local brothels....

One goal of legalized prostitution was to move prostituted women indoors into brothels and clubs where they would be allegedly less vulnerable than in street prostitution. However, many women are in street prostitution because they want to avoid being controlled and exploited by pimps (transformed in legalized systems into sex businessmen). Other women do not want to register or submit to health checks, as required by law in some countries where prostitution is legalized. Thus, legalization may actually *drive some women into* street prostitution. Arguing against an Italian proposal for legalized prostitution, Esohe Aghatise has suggested that brothels actually deprive women of what little protection they may have on the street, confining women to closed spaces where they have little chance of meeting outreach workers or others who might help them exit prostitution.

In the Netherlands, women in prostitution point out that legalization or decriminalization of the sex industry does not erase the stigma of prostitution. Because they must register and lose their anonymity, women are more vulnerable to being stigmatized as "whores," and this identity follows them everyplace. Thus, the majority of women in prostitution still operate illegally and underground. Some members of Parliament who originally supported the legalization of brothels on the grounds that this would liberate women are now seeing that legalization actually reinforces the oppression of women....

The argument that legalization was supposed to take the criminal elements out of sex businesses by strict regulation of the industry has failed. The real growth in prostitution in Australia since legalization took effect has been in the illegal sector. Over a period of 12 months from 1998–1999, unlicensed brothels in Victoria tripled in number and still operate with impunity. In New South Wales where brothels were decriminalized in 1995, the number of brothels in Sydney had tripled to 400–500 by 1999, with the vast majority having no license to advertise or operate. In response to widespread police corruption, control of illegal prostitution was removed from police jurisdiction and placed under the control of local councils and planning regulators. However, the local councils do not have the resources to investigate illegal brothel operators.

Increasing Child Prostitution

Another argument for legalizing prostitution in the Netherlands was that it would help end child prostitution. Yet child prostitution in the Netherlands has increased dramatically during the 1990s. The Amsterdam-based ChildRight organization estimates that the number of children in prostitution has increased by more than 300% between 1996–2001, going from 4,000 children in 1996 to 15,000 in 2001. ChildRight estimates that at least 5,000 of these children in Dutch prostitution are trafficked from other countries, with a large segment being Nigerian girls.

Child prostitution has increased dramatically in the state of Victoria compared to other Australian states where prostitution has not been legalized. Of all the states and territories in Australia, the highest number of reported incidences of child prostitution came from Victoria. In a 1998 study undertaken by ECPAT (End Child Prostitution and Trafficking), who conducted research for the Australian National Inquiry on Child Prostitution, there was increased evidence of organized commercial exploitation of children.

Prostitutes Are Not Protected

In two studies in which 186 victims of commercial sexual exploitation were interviewed, women consistently indicated that prostitution establishments did little to protect them, regardless of whether the establishments were legal or illegal. One woman said, "The only time they protect anyone is to protect the customers."

One of these studies interviewed 146 victims of trafficking in 5 countries. Eighty percent of the women interviewed had suffered physical violence from pimps and buyers and endured similar and multiple health effects from the violence and sexual exploitation, regardless of whether the women were trafficked internationally or were in local prostitution.

John Pritchett. © John Pritchett. Reproduced by permission.

A second study of women trafficked for prostitution in the United States yielded the following statements. Women who reported that sex businesses gave them some protection qualified it by pointing out that no "protector" was ever in the room with them. One woman who was in out-call prostitution stated: "The driver functioned as a bodyguard. You're supposed to call when you get in, to ascertain that everything was OK. But they are not standing outside the door while you're in there, so anything could happen". . . .

Making Women into Commodities

With the advent of legalization in countries that have decriminalized the sex industry, many men who previously would not have risked buying women for sex now see prostitution as acceptable. When legal barriers disappear, so too do the social and ethical barriers to treating women as sexual merchandise. Legalization of prostitution sends the message to new generations of men and boys that women are sexual commodities and that prostitution is harmless fun.

As men have a plethora of "sexual services" offered to them in prostitution, women must compete by engaging in anal sex, sex without condoms, bondage and domination and other acts demanded by buyers. Once prostitution is legalized, for example, women's reproductive capacities are sellable products. Some buyers find pregnancy a turn-on and demand breast milk in their sexual encounters with pregnant women.

In the State of Victoria in Australia, specialty brothels are provided for disabled men. State-employed caretakers (who are mostly women) must take these men to the brothels if they wish to go and literally facilitate their physical sexual acts. Advertisements line the highways of Victoria offering women as objects for sexual use. Businessmen are encouraged to hold their corporate meetings in clubs where owners supply naked women on the table at tea breaks and lunchtime. A Melbourne brothel owner stated that the client base was "well educated professional men, who visit during the day and then go home to their families." Women in relationships with men find that often the men in their lives are visiting the brothels and sex clubs.

Legalization Does Not Promote Women's Health

A legalized system of prostitution often mandates health checks and certification, but only for women and not for male buyers. Health examinations or tests for women but not men make no public health sense because monitoring prostituted women does not protect *them* from HIV/AIDS or STDs. This is not to advocate that both women in prostitution and male buyers should be checked. It is simply to point out the duplicity of a policy that implies, "We'll have safer sex and HIV/AIDS control if we examine the women under a regulated or decriminalized system of prostitution." Male buyers can and do originally transmit disease to the women they purchase.

It has been argued that legalized brothels or other "controlled" prostitution establishments protect women through enforceable condom policies. In one study, 47% of women in U.S. prostitution stated that men expected sex without a condom; 73% reported that men offered to pay more for sex without a condom; and 45% of women said that men became abusive if they insisted that men use condoms. Although certain sex businesses had rules that required men to wear condoms, men nonetheless attempted to have sex without condoms. One woman stated: "It's 'regulation' to wear a condom at the sauna, but negotiable between parties on the side. Most guys expected blow jobs without a condom." . . .

"Safety policies" in brothels did not protect women from harm. Where brothels allegedly monitored the buyers and employed "bouncers," women stated that they were injured by buyers and, at times, by brothel owners and their friends. Even when someone intervened to momentarily control buyers' abuse, women lived in a climate of fear. Although 60% of women reported that buyers had sometimes been prevented from abusing them, half of those same women answered that, nonetheless, they thought that they might be killed by one of their buyers.

Legalization Does Not Enhance Women's Choice

Most women in prostitution did not make a rational choice to enter prostitution from among a range of other options. They did not sit down one day and decide that they wanted to be prostitutes. They did not have other real options such as medicine, law, nursing or politics. Instead, their "options" were more in the realm of how to feed themselves and their children. Such choices are better termed survival strategies.

Rather than consenting to prostitution, a prostituted woman more accurately complies with the extremely limited options available to her. Her compliance is required by the fact of having to adapt to conditions of inequality that are set by the customer who pays her to do what he wants her to do. . . .

Finally, rather than cashing in on the economic profits of the sex industry by taxing it, governments could seize assets of sex businesses and then use these funds to provide real alternatives for women in prostitution. Measures to prevent trafficking and prostitution, or to prosecute traffickers, recruiters, pimps and buyers, will be inadequate unless governments invest in the futures of prostituted women by providing economic resources that enable women to improve their lives.

| "Making prostitution legal will allow the
act to be managed instead of ignored."

Prostitution Should Be Legalized

Mark Liberator

Rather than waste tax dollars trying to prevent prostitution, governments should legalize and regulate the practice, argues Mark Liberator in the following viewpoint. Prohibiting prostitution forces the industry underground, he claims, putting prostitutes and their customers at risk. If prostitution were legal, Liberator maintains, prostitutes would not be exploited and abused by pimps and organized crime bosses. Regulation would also control the spread of sexually transmitted diseases, he asserts, because prostitutes would be required to undergo regular medical examinations. Liberator, a high school mathematics teacher, publishes the e-magazine, the Liberator.

As you read, consider the following questions:

1. According to Liberator, what different strategies do countries use to handle prostitution?

2. What are the end results of penalizing prostitution, in the author's view?

3. In the author's opinion, how many teens are prostituted each year in the United States?

When we examine sex as a trade, the combination of philosophy, cultural precedence, religious influence and politics made each country select how to handle it in its own way. In Singapore, sex for money is open and commonplace. Denmark women can be legal prostitutes so long as it is not their sole means of income. Canada, France and Mexico allow it. Prostitutes must be contained within brothels in the Netherlands, unlike within England and Wales where prostitution is limited to individual providers. Israel, the historical stage for the Bible, allows it, too. Meanwhile, the United States has made prostitution illegal (misdemeanor) in all states, except certain counties of Nevada.

Even though it is quite natural on a biological level for males and females to host desires and have intimate relations with many partners it would probably be a very unproductive line of reasoning when considering the legalization of prostitution. Humankind no longer succumbs to animal behavior and has built infrastructures that depend on us expunging primitive mannerisms. Unlike the animal kingdom, we deal with sexuality without force. Nevertheless, there is still room for prostitution within civilized societies, since sex can be considered to be a service traded for goods, services, relationships, and money. . . .

The Benefits of Legalization

Most everywhere in the United States, our legal system penalizes prostitutes and their customers for what they do as consenting adults. Money is still spent on law enforcement efforts to catch prostitutes and their customers. Once caught, justice departments have to process these people through very expensive systems.

What are the end results? Police personnel and courtrooms are overburdened with these cases, having little or no impact on prostitution. The prostitutes and their customers pay their fines and are back to the streets in no time in a revolving door process. Catch and release may work for recreational fishing but it has no deterring effect on prostitution.

Making prostitution legal will allow the act to be managed instead of ignored. Pimps and organized crime figures, who regularly treat their workers on subhuman levels, would no longer control women. In some countries, prostitute rings buy and sell women on the black market, force their women to comply through violence and create unhealthy working conditions. When prostitutes operate independently and in secret, many times they become abused by their own customers.

Making the Invisible Visible

Legalizing prostitution would prevent underground prostitution that occurs today. When men want to pay for sex, they find prostitutes. These people work in massage parlors, escort services, strip bars and modeling agencies or still work corners as traditional streetwalkers. There are legitimate parlors, dating services, bars and agencies but of the hundreds that exist within newspaper classified advertisements and telephone directories, there are a large number that provide sexual services. A routine search through Google's Internet news engine for 'prostitution' routinely reveals connections between prostitution and these falsetto agencies.

It is estimated that 100,000 to 3 million teens are nearly invisibly prostituted per year in the United States. If we allow prostitution to remain hidden from view and basically invisible to the law as it is today, we allow a number of teens to be swept up into prostitution every year. When adult women decide to exchange money for sex, it is a personal choice open to them under the philosophy of a free, democratic society. When troubled minors who do not yet have the social survival skills decide to prostitute, they are often manipulated by opportunists who exploit these teens, typically leading to horrific ends. Legalizing prostitution will help prevent these instances through regulation.

Legalized, regulated prostitution has many benefits. Encounters can happen within controlled environments that bring about safety for both the customers and the prostitutes. Prostitutes would no longer be strong-armed by pimps or organized crime rings. Underage prostitution would be curtailed. There would also be health-safety improvements.

The Health and Safety Benefits

The status quo is a poor health-safety plan. With sexually transmitted diseases (STDs) like syphilis, gonorrhea, chlamydia and herpes, prostitutes must be monitored to prevent the spread of these afflictions. Chancroid, an STD typically found in third world nations, is occurring in places throughout the U.S. due to transmission brought on through illegal prostitution. Chancroid makes ulcers in the vagina that assist with the spread of HIV/AIDS. . . .

R. Steen cited a practical example of how government can help its citizens. It makes practical sense to monitor prostitution and what better way is there to monitor it than by legalizing it and regulating it? Legalization would require prostitutes to undergo regular medical examinations. STDs would be prevented from being spread as well as other communicable ailments like hepatitis and tuberculosis. It would also reduce gender violence, allow women to escape prostitution, if they so choose, and prevent women from becoming infertile as a consequence to obtaining certain STDs.

The Role of Government

Whether one is a liberal or conservative, Republican or Democrat, the role of government is to carry out necessary duties its citizens cannot perform. Politicians are elected to government positions to solve the problems countries face. Some Democratic politicians insist government should be designed to act as a safety net for people who need help, by providing citizens with various social programs including public safety and healthcare entitlements. Other Republican representatives believe in freedom of choice through responsible action and rather institute high standards in education and healthcare to enable citizens with opportunities. Libertarians feel compelled to ensure civil rights and allow citizens to be self-governing members of society.

In these cases, the issue of morality aside, it can be plainly seen how each political view contains strong elements supporting legalization. Maintaining the status quo has the U.S. throwing tax dollars away by spending it on law enforcement, criminal justice and prisons. The U.S. healthcare system is currently reactionary at best; it passively handles STDs after they occur instead of instituting mechanisms to prevent them from happening in the first place. . . .

The best way to understand the current state of affairs concerning prostitution is to entertain an analogy. Pretend government is a business. Politicians would be the managers and prostitution would be a certain procedure the company had to manage. Would a successful business ignore a procedure when it performed poorly? Would it allow a poor procedure to continue or would a successful business instead rethink its position and improve it? All successful companies must evolve over time if they are to stay in business and excel. Fortunately, the U.S. Constitution allows its citizens to view government like a dynamic business because it is a work in progress. Laws can change and adapt to meet the demands of a modern civilization. It is a far better strategy than hoping it will go away and clean up itself.

Where are the limits for two consenting adults in privacy? How government is shaped to handle that question will decide how women's rights, social programs, public healthcare, the safety of youth and possibly the general safety of citizens are valued. If moral obstacles prevent citizens from obtaining a government that helps its people while preserving freedoms, then a paradigm shift must be considered. A movement away

Recognizing the Rights of Adults

Legalizing prostitution would not be a moral endorsement of paid sex, any more than the 1st Amendment is a moral endorsement of supermarket tabloids. It would just be a recognition of the right of adults to make their own choices about sins of the flesh—and of the eternal futility of trying to stop them.

Steve Chapman, Chicago Tribune, *July 14, 2005.*

from values that are harmful is difficult only if one decides to cling to outdated, self-destructive traditions.

Politicians should be careful how they address the philosophical limits of adult privacy. A number of people believe government should have no right deciding how adults conduct their sexual lives, even when an exchange of money is involved. . . .

Answering the Critics

The critics of legalized prostitution insist sex for money is wrong because it is harmful to prostitutes. They claim prostitutes are victims of physical abuse and frequently suffer from homelessness, alcoholism and dependency on other drugs. These critics report that prostitutes have often been sexually and/or physically abused while growing up.

What critics do not report is a plan to help these workers. Their rationale is a status quo model, which does absolutely nothing to help these women. Instead of managing the problem through the medical and social interventions accompanied by regulation of the industry, critics of legalized prostitution would rather adopt prohibition and cold abandonment.

When critics mention neighborhood safety, they do not offer meaningful alternatives. Their plan is to heighten police patrols, encourage undercover sting operations, and stiffen penalties. . . . [Prohibition] drives the industry further underground, making it harder to stop the spread of HIV/AIDS and various other sexually transmitted diseases in a community.

If critics of prostitution wanted to truly help prostitutes and the neighborhoods where prostitution occurs, they would reconsider their position. Prohibitionists retain their view as a result of moral codes, not because of unbiased scientific study. Research shows the many benefits of legalization. Allowing prohibitionist propaganda to drive laws and the way civil liberties are viewed will guarantee: drug dependency will not be abated, physical abuse will continue, and STDs will spread. Most important, the women who need help will continue their lives on the same harmful paths. . . .

Drawing Conclusions

Sexual relations are handled differently in countries around the world. Most countries encourage varied forms of monogamy, others polygyny [the practice of having more than one wife]. Even in the case of monogamy, there are numerous countries that impose no restrictions on prostitution, unlike a majority of the communities within the United States. . . .

The implementation of [the] prohibition [of alcohol] was a result of an abolitionist philosophy and caused great harm to the country through lost taxes, increased crime rates and higher suicide rates. Similarly, when the U.S. abandoned its abolitionist stand on abortion, the country benefited from fewer deaths from botched back alley abortions. This proved prohibitionist thinking to be baseless and actually detrimental to communities.

There are many benefits to legalized prostitution. The benefits include (1) allowing law enforcement agencies to respond to more important crimes, (2) freeing justice systems from nuisance cases, (3) helping women who are trapped by prostitution, and (4) preventing teens from being ensnared into prostitution.

When data from countries that ban prostitution is compared with data from countries that do not, many startling discoveries can be observed. Countries without anti-prostitution laws have less murders, less rapes, and prosecute/imprison less people. HIV/AIDS is less of a problem; suicide rates are lower as are divorce rates, too.

Critics of the legalization of prostitution offer no alternative to a troublesome problem. These people would rather adopt the status quo model, which virtually abandons lower strata, low socio-economic prostitutes. Instead of managing the problem, these critics view the continued downward spiral of this subgroup as acceptable.

The critics of legalized prostitution rest comfortably within relatively new moral codes. The religions that now reject prostitution once used to manage it. However, even though religionists publicly denounce prostitution, too many hypocritically entertain like services and commit adultery. The Catholic Church has covered up institutional pedophilia at the expense of demeaning religious values and the lives of those who aspire to follow them.

Enlightened people within civilized societies pride themselves on the contributions made to others who are less fortunate. Low strata prostitutes clearly rest within the domain of the less fortunate, but the countries who cling to anti-prostitution laws choose to abandon these people and thereby negatively affect the crime, health, and general safety of those nations. One must reconsider whether or not those countries are truly civilized.

> "As a result of the prostitution-trafficking
> link ... no U.S. grant funds should be
> awarded to foreign non-governmental
> organizations that support legal state-
> regulated prostitution."

U.S. Policies Will Reduce Sex Trafficking

U.S. Department of State

To reduce the trafficking of women and children into sexual sla-
very, claims the U.S. Department of State in the following view-
point, the United States should not grant funds to organizations
that support legalized prostitution. Prostitution, the authors
maintain, is a dangerous and dehumanizing practice that threat-
ens the health and well-being of women and children. The legal-
ization of prostitution does not protect women and children
trapped in prostitution, the authors argue. In fact, the authors
claim, sex trafficking has increased in countries where prostitu-
tion is legal.

As you read, consider the following questions:

1. According to the U.S. Department of State, what percentage of women and children are among those trafficked each year?

2. What has field research in nine countries concluded
   about prostitution, in the author's view?

U.S. Department of State, "The Link Between Prostitution and Sex Trafficking," November 24, 2004.

3. In the author's opinion, how does legalization create a safe haven for criminals who traffic people into prostitution?

The U.S. Government adopted a strong position against legalized prostitution in a December 2002 National Security Presidential Directive based on evidence that prostitution is inherently harmful and dehumanizing, and fuels trafficking in persons, a form of modern-day slavery.

Prostitution and related activities—including pimping and patronizing or maintaining brothels—fuel the growth of modern-day slavery by providing a façade behind which traffickers for sexual exploitation operate.

Where prostitution is legalized or tolerated, there is a greater demand for human trafficking victims and nearly always an increase in the number of women and children trafficked into commercial sex slavery.

Of the estimated 600,000 to 800,000 people trafficked across international borders annually, 80 percent of victims are female, and up to 50 percent are minors. Hundreds of thousands of these women and children are used in prostitution each year.

The vast majority of women in prostitution don't want to be there. Few seek it out or choose it, and most are desperate to leave it. A 2003 study first published in the scientific *Journal of Trauma Practice* found that 89 percent of women in prostitution want to escape. And children are also trapped in prostitution—despite the fact that international covenants and protocols impose upon state parties an obligation to criminalize the commercial sexual exploitation of children.

Prostitution Is Inherently Harmful

Few activities are as brutal and damaging to people as prostitution. Field research in nine countries concluded that 60–75 percent of women in prostitution were raped, 70–95 percent were physically assaulted, and 68 percent met the criteria for post traumatic stress disorder in the same range as treatment-seeking combat veterans and victims of state-organized torture. Beyond this shocking abuse, the public health implications of prostitution are devastating and include a myriad of serious and fatal diseases, including HIV/AIDS.

A path-breaking, five-country academic study concluded that research on prostitution has overlooked "[t]he burden of physical injuries and illnesses that women in the sex industry sustain from the violence inflicted on them, or from their significantly higher rates of hepatitis B, higher risks of cervical cancer, fertility complications, and psychological trauma."

State attempts to regulate prostitution by introducing medical check-ups or licenses don't address the core problem: the routine abuse and violence that form the prostitution experience and brutally victimize those caught in its netherworld. Prostitution leaves women and children physically, mentally, emotionally, and spiritually devastated. Recovery takes years, even decades—often, the damage can never be undone.

Prostitution Creates a Safe Haven for Criminals

Legalization of prostitution expands the market for commercial sex, opening markets for criminal enterprises and creating a safe haven for criminals who traffic people into prostitution. Organized crime networks do not register with the government, do not pay taxes, and do not protect prostitutes. Legalization simply makes it easier for them to blend in with a purportedly regulated sex sector and makes it more difficult for prosecutors to identify and punish those who are trafficking people.

The Swedish Government has found that much of the vast profit generated by the global prostitution industry goes into the pockets of human traffickers. The Swedish Government

The Price of Nonjudgmental Action

U.S. leadership in [the fight against trafficking] is needed because many of the world's humanitarian organizations have been willing to overlook and excuse the trade in women and children. The reason is as simple as it is tragic: The sex slaves are a high-risk group for HIV infection. Unfortunately, efforts to curb the global HIV/AIDS crisis have led to "nonjudgmental" condom distribution campaigns that ignore some of the world's worst crimes and human rights violations. Indeed, the HIV/AIDS prevention educators often make deals with perpetrators.

Donna M. Hughes, Weekly Standard, *February 24, 2003.*

said, "International trafficking in human beings could not flourish but for the existence of local prostitution markets where men are willing and able to buy and sell women and children for sexual exploitation."

To fight human trafficking and promote equality for women, Sweden has aggressively prosecuted customers, pimps, and brothel owners since 1999. As a result, two years after the new policy, there was a 50 percent decrease in women prostituting and a 75 percent decrease in men buying sex. Trafficking for the purposes of sexual exploitation decreased as well. In contrast, where prostitution has been legalized or tolerated, there is an increase in the demand for sex slaves and the number of victimized foreign women—many likely victims of human trafficking.

As a result of the prostitution-trafficking link, the U.S. government concluded that no U.S. grant funds should be awarded to foreign non-governmental organizations that support legal state-regulated prostitution. Prostitution is not the oldest profession, but the oldest form of oppression.

| "U.S. interventions around the world are contributing to the trafficking and exploitation of women."

U.S. Policies Promote Sex Trafficking

Eartha Melzer

According to Eartha Melzer in the following viewpoint, the Trafficking Victims Protection Act, which sets standards for all nations to meet in combating human trafficking, is ineffective. Commercial exploitation of women worldwide has increased, she claims, and much of the rise is due to U.S.-led wars in Afghanistan and Iraq. U.S. military personnel increase the number of customers seeking prostitution, according to Melzer. Moreover, by denying funds to overseas programs that do not come out against prostitution, the act undermines the efforts of those helping women protect themselves from disease and violence. Melzer writes for the Washington Blade, *a weekly newspaper for Washington, D.C.'s gay community.*

As you read, consider the following questions:

1. In Melzer's opinion, what has overshadowed the economic plight of women who sell sex for money?
2. What other Bush administration policies oppose harm reduction strategies, in the author's view?

Eartha Melzer, "Trafficking in Politics," *In These Times,* March 14, 2005. Reproduced by permission of the publisher, www.inthesetimes.com.

3. According to the author, what do Tier 3 countries have in common?

[P]resident] George W. Bush seems to take one human rights campaign seriously—he decries human trafficking as "modern slavery" and a "special evil." Indeed, he used sex slavery to mobilize his evangelical base during the 2004 campaign.

The evangelicals are not alone. In 2000, they formed an uncommon coalition with feminist groups to lobby for a new law combating human trafficking. The resulting Trafficking Victims Protection Act (TVPA) set up minimum standards for all countries to meet in combating trafficking, and created the Office to Monitor and Combat Trafficking in Persons within the State Department.

But four years into the anti-trafficking program, both evangelicals and feminists are disappointed with the results. Commercial sexual exploitation of women is on the rise globally, and in many cases the United States is driving, not stopping, the trend. Countries with the most severe trafficking problems have been ignored, while others appear to have been targeted for political reasons. And the economic plight of women who sell sex for money has been overshadowed by a sensationalized rhetoric of sin and redemption.

A Simplistic Take on a Complex Problem

Regulating the global sex trade is no easy proposition. Prostitution is legal, with various caveats, in several countries, and international legal experts have developed elaborate definitions to distinguish between victims of coercion and adults who willingly exchange sex for money. The International Labour Organization, discussing the booming sex trade in Asia, recognizes, "In many cases, sex work is often the only viable alternative for women in communities coping with poverty, unemployment, failed marriages and family obligations in nearly complete absence of social welfare programs."

Bush, however, has eschewed the notion that sex workers have needs or agency, instead lumping together trafficking, prostitution and commercial sex as offenses against the "moral law that stands above nations." With the 2003 National Security Directive 22, Bush announced a "zero tolerance" policy for trafficking, including involvement in trafficking by U.S. service members. The directive also required that anti-trafficking funds be kept from groups that do not take an abolitionist approach to prostitution.

As with the administration's policies on illegal drugs, family planning and AIDS, the U.S. policy against trafficking does not focus on harm reduction. Funding preference is given to groups that forcibly remove women from prostitution. That means leaving out some of the organizations best situated to address problems faced by sex workers, like the Sonagachi project in India. This health project, for and by sex workers, has been recognized by the United Nations as a model program for stopping the spread of HIV and protecting the rights of people involved in the sex trade.

The Bush administration's absolutist approach bears strong similarities to American moral crusades of days past. In the early 20th century, industrialization and immigration fueled sensational stories of "defiled virgins," and a crusade against prostitution resulted in the 1910 passage of the White Slavery Traffic Act, which banned transporting women across state lines for "immoral purposes."

Nearly a century later, the media is rife with accounts that similarly depend on public prurience and stereotypes of women as victims. On January 25, 2004, the *New York Times Magazine* ran a cover story by Peter Landesman titled "Sex Slaves on Main Street: the Girls Next Door." While this tale of large-scale trafficking of women and girls into the United States was quickly discredited, that didn't stop director Roland

Defunding Successful Strategies

Holly Burkhalter of Physicians for Human Rights asserts that forcing an indigenous NGO [nongovernmental organization] in a developing country to oppose prostitution before it can qualify for U.S. government support to fight HIV/AIDS "could end up defunding some of the most successful HIV/AIDS prevention services and empowerment strategies for women in the sex industry." In an op-ed in *The Washington Post*, Burkhalter writes: "One such group's representative, describing her effort to help Bangladeshi brothel workers acquire the right to wear shoes or sandals outside of brothels—a simple dignity denied them by local custom—stated: 'How can we help these beaten down, marginalized women organize themselves to achieve such victories if we are publicly opposing what they do to earn money?'"

Susan A. Cohen, Guttmacher Report on Public Policy, *February 2005.*

Emmerich, the man who brought us [the film] *Independence Day*, from optioning the film rights.

Double Standards

Under TVPA, the Department of Justice (DOJ) has set up Human Trafficking Task Forces in cities around the country. A November 2004 DOJ press release, announcing a $450,000 anti-trafficking grant to the D.C. Metro Police Department's "highly experienced" prostitution unit, stated that the money would be used to arrest prostitutes and "work up the chain to apprehend traffickers."

Such an approach not only conflates human trafficking and prostitution, but could further persecute people working in the sex industry. Taina Bien-Aime, executive director of the

New York-based feminist group Equality Now, explains that while TVPA provides for visas for trafficked women, in order to avoid prosecution and deportation any undocumented immigrant must cooperate in the prosecution of her trafficker. Obtaining this cooperation may prove difficult because the trafficked women are often from the same village as the trafficker and many fear repercussions to their families.

American prosecution of these crimes abroad seems decidedly less aggressive. The State Department has a mandate from Congress to issue annual Trafficking in Persons (TIP) reports grading countries on their progress in stopping trafficking. "Tier 3" countries—those judged by the United States not to be making progress—face sanctions.

According to a source at the State Department, most Tier 3 countries are the ones that have poor relations with the U.S. government, such as North Korea, Cuba and Venezuela. Venezuela's ranking, for example, seems based more on its refusal to recognize the U.S. program than with the scope of trafficking there.

The selective attention to the seriousness of some countries' trafficking has angered conservatives. Gary Haugen is the director of International Justice Mission (IJM), a Christian group that has received millions of dollars in federal funds to work on trafficking. IJM infiltrates the sex trade in India and Thailand and conducts brothel raids, placing sex workers in homes for rescue and re-education.

In June 2002, Haugen told the Congressional Human Rights Caucus that "the State Department has rendered the standards of the act virtually meaningless," by placing India and Thailand in Tier 2. Although the sex trade is huge in these countries, Haugen said, virtually no one has been prosecuted for trafficking.

Adding Injury to Insult

Even worse, U.S. interventions around the world are contributing to the trafficking and exploitation of women. The State

Department TIP report for 2003 noted that trafficking activities have increased in Afghanistan and Iraq as a consequence of instability brought on by armed conflict.

"As we have seen elsewhere," the report stated, "the demand for prostitution often increases with the presence of military troops, expatriates and international personnel who have access to disposable income."

On April 24, 2002, Ben Johnston, a helicopter mechanic for DynCorp in Bosnia, testified to Congress about DynCorp employees who were allegedly buying women and girls to keep in their homes as sex slaves. Yet, despite the president's "zero tolerance" directive and the development of laws that would hold contractors responsible for involvement in sex trafficking, DynCorp remains in good standing as a U.S. contractor, and in 2003 was awarded a no-bid contract to "reestablish police, justice and prison functions in post-conflict Iraq."

In 2002, media reports detailed how "courtesy patrol" units around U.S. bases in Korea were directing soldiers and tourists to locations where they could engage the services of sex workers, mainly women from Russia and the Philippines who were held captive and forced to have sex with soldiers. South Korean authorities estimated that their country's sex industry was worth $22 billion a year and involved 330,000 women.

The Fog of Moral Relativism

Congress called for an investigation and on September 21, 2004, the House Armed Services Committee and the Commission on Security and Cooperation in Europe held a forum titled "Enforcing U.S. Policies Against Trafficking in Persons: How is the U.S. Military Doing?"

The inspector general of the Defense Department, Joseph E. Schmitz, a Bush appointee charged with being the "eyes, ears and conscience of the Defense Department" on trafficking issues, failed to give specific information about his investigation. Instead, he delivered a paper at the hearing called "Examining Sex Slavery Through the Fog of Moral Relativism," which read in part:

> Whatever else one might say about sex slavery in the 21st century, these recent proactive measures taken by U.S. and Western leaders reaffirm the "moral truth" that prostitution and human trafficking fall within those "dissolute and immoral practices" envisioned by our Continental Congress when it prescribed a duty to "guard against and suppress" such practices through, *inter alia*, vigilance by leaders in "inspecting the conduct of all persons who are placed under their command."

At the same hearing, the duty of substantive analysis fell to lawyer Martina Vanderberg, a former researcher with Human Rights Watch. In contrast to Schmitz's—and Bush's—bombastic pronouncements, she testified that the loopholes for contractors have not been closed, that education programs have not yet yielded the participation of soldiers in identifying traffickers and that it is unclear how the zero tolerance policy is being implemented.

| "*Customers were the most frequently identified perpetrators of violence across all types of prostitution venues.*"

Laws That Target Customers Will Protect Prostitutes

Darla Mueller

In the following viewpoint Darla Mueller contends that johns are responsible for most of the violence against prostitutes. Despite this fact, Mueller maintains, many more prostitutes are arrested and convicted than are johns. The programs that most effectively curb the demand for prostitutes and help protect them from abuse are those that criminalize johns and decriminalize prostitutes, she asserts. Mueller writes for Homeward Bound, *a publication of the Chicago Coalition for the Homeless.*

As you read, consider the following questions:

1. According to Mueller, what is survival sex?
2. What role do johns play in recruiting youth and women in the sex trade, in the author's view?
3. In the author's opinion, why is it difficult to determine if john schools are effective?

Darla Mueller, "Curbing the Demand for Prostitution," *Homeward Bound,* Fall 2005. Reproduced by permission.

Runaway youth and homeless women often fall prey to a dangerous life of prostitution. A 2003 study conducted by CCH [Chicago Coalition for the Homeless] found that 50 percent of women involved in prostitution had experienced homelessness. Many women and youth have engaged in survival sex, which is the exchange of sex for money, food, shelter, and other basic needs. Others become homeless or struggle to avoid it when they exit the sex trade, often the only means of support they have known.

Even if we ensure that services, housing, and job opportunities are accessible and available to survivors of prostitution, the problems inherent in the sex trade will remain unsolved if the demand side is not addressed.

Fueling the Sex Trade

The customers of prostitution, otherwise known as "johns," who fuel the sex trade are seldom the target of law enforcement crackdowns in Chicago. The evidence lies in the arrest statistics: In 2004, Chicago police arrested 3,204 prostitutes but only 950 johns.

Conviction rates are even less equitable. Between 2000 and 2002, 388 persons were convicted of felony prostitution in Cook County [Illinois]. In that time period, no felony convictions were handed down for solicitation. Though prostitution and solicitation are misdemeanor offenses, a person is eligible, upon the second misdemeanor conviction, for a felony upgrade requiring state prison time and/or supervision. In practice, customers rarely receive this upgrade or face prison or jail time. While both prostitution and solicitation have the same penalties under Illinois law, no parity exists in practice.

The violence and other predatory behaviors perpetrated by johns necessitate addressing a deeper issue. According to a 2002 study of women involved in prostitution in metropolitan Chicago, customers were the most frequently identified perpetrators of violence across all types of prostitution venues. Johns often play a significant role in recruiting and maintaining youth and women in the sex trade, particularly by luring runaways and exploiting survival needs such as shelter, food, or money.

This paper will describe efforts to deter customers of prostitution locally, in other parts of the country, and abroad. It will also explore what is known of the effectiveness of these various strategies.

Examining Local Strategies

In Chicago, upon arrest customers can be charged with either a City Ordinance or a State Misdemeanor charge. The city charge allows for the customer's car to be impounded while the State Charge allows for a Class A or B misdemeanor conviction with possible jail or prison time, community service or agency referral. Upon conviction under the city charge, the offender pays an administrative fine between $750–$1,500 to retrieve his or her car. Although customers can be charged initially with a state and city violation, they can only be prosecuted for one of the two. In addition, as part of a new deterrence initiative introduced by Mayor [Richard M.] Daley in June 2005, upon arrest, a customer's name, half address, and mug shot are placed online on the Chicago Police Department's website for 30 days.

Educational programs, or "john schools," are another deterrence strategy used in various cities such as Washington, D.C.; West Palm Beach, Florida; Pittsburgh; Buffalo; and Brooklyn, New York. Recently Chicago has developed a john school, offered by Genesis House. Persons charged with solicitation can opt to go to john school as a condition of probation. Tuition is charged, and fees collected for the eight-hour seminar go back to Genesis House, which provides services to women involved in prostitution.

Typically, john schools offer a day of education covering various topics:

- A review of prostitution laws

- Facts and statistics about prostitution and pimping

- Physical health risks and treatment

- Testimony from survivors or advocates about the victimization and hardship of a prostitute's life

- Consequences of john behavior to themselves, their families, and their communities

- Concepts about relationships and sex addiction

In addition to attending the school, offenders must not reoffend for a period of time to avoid a court trial and incarceration.

San Francisco's model program, the First Offender Prostitution Program (FOPP), has a multilayered approach. The City arrests johns, who then attend john school. The fees collected from the men who participate in the john school fund comprehensive intervention services for women and girls involved in prostitution. Participants in FOPP have completed surveys indicating evidence of change both in attitude toward prostitution and in future behavior.

Another john school, part of Toronto's Diversion Program, did pre- and postprogram surveys with 366 men who had attended. The surveys showed increased awareness of Canadian prostitution laws and the dangers associated with prostitution, as well as a decrease in likelihood to support the legalization of prostitution.

Although john schools report very low recidivism for the participants, recidivism rates are generally low for men arrested for solicitation, regardless of john school attendance. Thus, determining whether john schools are an effective intervention tool is difficult. Many customers are caught and arrested by female cops acting as decoys. Low recidivism rates may suggest that johns become more cautious once they've been arrested or have attended john school, avoiding decoy cops and/or soliciting sex in less public areas or from organized "indoor" sex trade venues such as strip clubs.

Another strategy used to deter johns involves public shaming. As of June 2005, the Chicago Police Department hosts a website that displays photos and identifying information of arrested johns. Police in Akron, Ohio, launched a similar website in 2003. In Denver and Kansas City, johns' information is displayed on cable public access channels. Identifying information appears on billboards in Oakland, California, and Omaha, Nebraska. The effectiveness of public shaming tactics targeting johns is questionable, with many of these jurisdictions providing mixed results. CCH does not support the city's use of a "john website" as a deterrence strategy.

Looking at International Strategies

In other parts of the world (and in some counties in Nevada), elements of prostitution and solicitation are legal. For example, in the Netherlands and Germany, prostitution and solicitation are legal and the government regulates the industry and collects taxes from business operations such as brothels. A 2003 University of London study (sponsored by the Scottish government) examined the outcomes of prostitution policies in Australia, Ireland, the Netherlands, and Sweden, countries where prostitution has been legalized or regulated in different ways. In the first three countries, the results showed substantial increases in all facets of the sex industry, in the involvement of organized crime, in child prostitution, and especially in the number of foreign women and girls trafficked into the region. The results also indicated an increase in violence against women.

Sweden, however, went further to address the problem than simply legalizing it. Sweden passed a law in 1999 criminalizing the buyers of commercial sex acts and decriminalizing the sellers of sex acts. Prostitution was denounced as "an aspect of male violence against women and children," and the government increased funding both toward services to help women exit the sex trade and toward public education. Police and prosecutors were trained intensively and pushed to enforce the law. Within five years, Sweden drastically reduced the number of both women in prostitution and johns. Stockholm saw reductions between 60 and 80 percent; other cities have almost completely rid themselves of street prostitution and are seeing massage parlors and brothels steadily disappear. In addition, Sweden has been able to almost completely cut out the trafficking of foreign women and girls into the country. In 2002, Sweden passed legislation increasing the government's law enforcement capabilities targeting recruiters, transporters, and hosts involved in human trafficking

The CCH-led Prostitution Alternatives Roundtable (PART) has been working intensively over the past two years with the Mayor's Office on Domestic Violence and various other entities to assess the way prostitution is dealt with in Chicago. A series of recommendations are being developed, several pertaining to deterring johns.

As part of a large-scale public awareness campaign and a means to deter johns, PART has partnered with Beyondmedia and Chicago Legal Advocacy for Incarcerated Mothers (CLAIM) to produce a film about the sex trade with a group of 13 survivors of prostitution.

Additionally, PART is working with Dr. Melissa Farley of Prostitution Research & Education to conduct groundbreaking research in Chicago with customers of the sex trade. The research will help us to understand their motivations and practices and will ultimately serve to inform our advocacy and identify better deterrence strategies.

Finally, PART supports putting more resources into enforcement of current anti-trafficking and anti-solicitation laws as a strategy to reduce demand and exploitation.

| "An enforcement approach that targets
clients as well as sex workers ... could
exacerbate conditions for sex workers."

Laws That Target Customers Harm Prostitutes

Rosie Campbell and Merl Storr

*While laws that punish both clients and prostitutes may appear
to be more equitable than those focused only on prostitutes, they
are harmful to women, claim sex work researchers Rosie Campbell and Merl Storr in the following viewpoint. Targeting customers reduces a prostitute's client base and forces prostitutes to
engage in risky behaviors, such as not using a condom in order
to compete with other prostitutes, the authors maintain. Moreover, they assert, prostitutes' exposure to violent, criminally in-
clined clients increases because these men are less likely to be dis-
couraged by legal penalties than are upstanding men with
families and careers to protect. Campbell conducts research at
the Applied Research Centre at Liverpool Hope University College. Storr is a sociology professor at the University of East London.*

As you read, consider the following questions:

1. How do Campbell and Storr explain the shift to laws
   that also punish the men who pay for sex?

Rosie Campbell and Merl Storr, "Challenging the Kerb Crawler Rehabilitation Programme," *Feminist Review,* Spring 2001, pp. 94-108. Reproduced with permission of
Palgrave Macmillan.

2. What is wrong with a discourse that dehumanizes the clients of prostitutes, in the authors' view?

3. According to the authors, what impact does having fewer clients have on a prostitute's client negotiations?

In the United States, Canada and some European countries many feminists have become increasingly critical of responses to street prostitution that concentrate solely on punishing women who sell sex while ignoring their male clients. In order to address this gender imbalance some feminists have advocated the enforcement and/or strengthening of kerb crawling [streetwalking] legislation and other schemes that target men who pay for sex. During 1998–9 one initiative which aimed to target men who pay for sex in the UK [United Kingdom], the Kerb Crawler Rehabilitation Programme (KCRP), was piloted in Leeds, West Yorkshire. The KCRP was established as a pilot project set up by the Research Centre for Violence, Abuse and Gender Relations at Leeds Metropolitan University in conjunction with West Yorkshire Police. This programme intended to shift the focus from the women who sell sex—specifically, in this case, street-working women—to the men who pay. The programme aimed 'to create safety in communities by adopting a more pro-active approach to kerb crawlers through shifting the focus from street prostitutes to the users'. . . .

Shifting the Balance?

Many policy makers, feminists, sex worker activists and resident communities affected by street prostitution have become frustrated with the existing 'traditional' legal management of street prostitution in the UK. Crudely summarized, this has involved responding to residential complaints by enforcing the soliciting legislation that relies upon arresting, prosecuting, fining and hence ultimately criminalizing street sex workers. . . .

However, a significant shift in focus, to include men who pay for sex as well as women who sell sex, has . . . begun. This shift has been discernible in both North America and Europe. Perhaps most indicative of this approach are the recent changes in legislation in Sweden, where in 1998 buying sex entered the penal code and the purchasing of sexual services was criminalized. [W.] McElroy refers to a 'sea change' in the way police authorities in the United States and Canada address street prostitution: this has entailed a shift towards a greater emphasis on arresting clients than was previously the case. . . .

While there is no doubt that an enforcement approach that targets clients as well as sex workers is more even-handed, it does not deliver a radically different approach but rather works within and reinforces the criminalization of prostitution. It is doubtful whether such an approach would see any fundamental benefits for sex workers; indeed, as we argue below, it could exacerbate conditions for sex workers. Fundamentally equalization does not address a legal framework that criminalizes sex workers, and addresses neither the issues faced by sex workers nor those of local residential communities affected by street prostitution.

Invisible Men

It is clear, then, as proponents of the KCRP themselves pointed out, that 'traditionally everyone with an interest in prostitution—health workers, researchers, police officers—have focused on women.' Although the research base regarding clients of sex workers is growing, it is still under-developed. There is great scope for feminist researchers to learn more about clients and to develop evidence-based proposals for positive policy interventions with this group. There is certainly a need to make the 'invisible men' involved in purchasing sex more visible within research, academic debates and policy consideration. So perhaps one beneficial outcome of the piloting of the KCRP was the high-profile publicity and public debate about clients it stimulated.

193

Yet it is questionable whether the language used to describe clients in reportage associated with the KCRP was helpful in enabling the discussion about clients to move beyond mythology and stereotypes. . . .

A discourse that constructs clients as dehumanized, dirty and animalistic gets us no nearer to an informed debate about clients, and perpetuates stereotypes that obscure the complex social, economic and cultural relationships in which commercial sex takes place. [C. Atkinson, L. Fraser, and J. Lowman] describe how research on clients has shifted from early work that treated the client as an abnormal deviant, through to more recent research that locates the client within cultural, gendered and economic relations. Much of the media discourse surrounding the KCRP appears to take us back to the construction of the client as an abnormal deviant. . . .

[M.] O'Neill [and S. Johnson, M. McDonald, and H. McGregor] stress the importance of including sex workers in debates about policy development. They emphasize the need to listen to and include women's experiences and voices, and they advocate woman-centred, multi-agency responses that include sex workers in developing policy and services. But in the development of the KCRP there appeared to have been only limited consultation with women who sell sex on the streets, or with the projects working with them. A crucial lesson for feminists to consider when involving themselves in policy development is the potential impact of policy on sex workers and the need to consult sex workers about their own needs and views. Initiatives which treat sex workers as *objects* of concern rather than as subjects—no matter how well intentioned—sit uneasily with feminist politics.

Policing and Sex Worker Safety

Projects such as the KCRP rely on the allocation of significant policing resources to the ongoing targeting of clients in order to 'recruit' clients into the school. Even if the focus is shifted

The Realities of the Demand Side

Men who pay for sex, far from being a tiny minority of men, are a substantial subsection of the male population, and broadly representative of it on most demographic variables. . . .

Whatever observers imagine client motivations to be, research findings indicate that clients themselves think their behaviour is largely about otherwise unmet sexual needs, which they are unable or unwilling to fulfill in emotionally significant relationships. These are the realities of the demand side. . . . Since sex behaviour is notoriously difficult to change, it is likely that the demand for commercial sex will persist, despite police enforcement and social disapproval.

United Kingdom Network of Sex Work Projects,
"Response to 'Paying the Price,'" November 26, 2004.

to clients, the active policing of street prostitution has a number of implications for the safety and welfare of street workers themselves.

First, it is crucial to point out that although a police force may decide to have a police operation that primarily targets clients, this does not give an amnesty to sex workers themselves. Hence police operations that proactively target clients usually involve the ongoing policing of female soliciting. More intensive policing operations mean that women are more likely to work in more isolated, unfamiliar and unsafe areas to avoid police surveillance and arrest. There may even be increased migration between 'beats' in different cities and towns where women are less familiar with the scene . . . in that area. Such patterns have been found in other cities where intensive police actions are enacted.

If there is an awareness that the police are looking for evidence of kerb crawling, the client and sex worker will be under pressure to ensure that the solicitation negotiation is as short as possible. Indeed numerous researchers have commented on this effect of contemporary legislation: that the limited time sex workers have to 'suss' out [investigate] clients and put in place safety strategies is further eroded.

One objective of the KCRP was to reduce the client base: the argument was that without demand there would be no supply. So what does a reduced client base mean for street sex workers? Fewer clients means women have to work extended hours to earn the sums of money they require for their subsistence (which may include drug-use). Increased competition for clients between sex workers means prices are depressed. There is likely to be a shift to later hours of working, to avoid police and to make contact with clients. This may also be combined with earlier hours of working in order to tap into a broader market of clients; earlier working in daytime hours can create more conflict with residents. This Leeds streetworker describes what she sees as the direct negative impact of the policing attached to the KCRP initiative on the context in which she sells sex:

> It used to be £20 for straight sex in a car but now the going rate is £10. I used to be out from 7–10.30 p.m. and could earn £130. Now I can be out from 5 p.m. until midnight and I might go home with just £40. It's too easy for men to get caught on the well-lit main roads now, so we're forced into dark side streets where we can't take number plates or get a good look at a client before we decide whether or not he is safe to get in the car with. And there's a lot of tension and hostility between the women that just wasn't there before. . . .

The Impact on Sexual Health

A growing body of UK research examining safer sexual practices among sex workers indicates that in commercial sex encounters rates of condom use are high. Yet research shows that with greater competition for clients and no alternative income, women are more likely to accept less money and take greater risks in terms of their personal safety and sexual health. . . .

The pressures reduce women's power to negotiate safer sex and hence they are more likely to sell unprotected sex. Initiatives targeting clients add another factor into this already difficult environment and create conditions where the pressures to take risks are heightened. Fewer clients mean greater competition between sex workers: this undermines sex worker power in negotiations with clients. In such a climate women may be more likely to 'take risks' in terms of condom use and other safe sex practices. [S.] Wilcock found that among those sex workers who disclosed that they had not used condoms, 'desperation for money and lack of clients were cited as the main reasons for not using condoms.' This would suggest that 'initiatives which aim to reduce client numbers by intensive policing and client arrest, and which do not make any other provision to meet sex workers' needs, carry serious health and safety implications.'

Challenging Violent Clients?

The high levels of violence faced by street sex workers have been widely noted. Such research indicates that only a minority of violent offences experienced by sex workers are reported to the police. Developing a policing approach and other policies that address the safety of sex workers is clearly a pressing priority. . . .

However, there is no clear evidence that the programme reduced violence against sex workers or had any impact on violent clients. Men who came to the KCRP had committed kerb crawling offences: they were not necessarily perpetrators of violence against sex workers. Whether the men who attended the school had been or would be violent towards sex workers was not known. Indeed the programme made it clear that it would not deal with men who were known to have committed violent offences. There is no evidence that all men who pay for sex will all be or will become violent and abusive towards sex workers. Such a 'scatter gun' approach only makes sense in an ideological framework in which all clients are treated as abusers. It does not allow for differences between clients in terms of their attitude towards and interaction with sex workers. . . .

Similar concerns have been raised by women involved in prostitution in North America. In the context of the Johns Schools in the USA, McElroy notes:

> The dozens of prostitutes I've spoken with are appalled by the development. One of their arguments is that the Johns School is making the streets less safe for prostitutes. The force of such laws will not determine, and historically has never determined, how many women have turned to the streets. But, prostitute activists argue, the laws will discourage a certain class of men from seeking out streetwalkers. Men who are married, with respectable careers and a reputation to protect, will not risk being publicly exposed as a john. On the other hand men who are criminally inclined towards prostitution will not be discouraged by the prospect of a police fine. Thus police/feminist policy keeps peaceful johns off the streets and leaves women to compete more vigorously for johns and screen less rigorously those who approach them. Is it any wonder that violence against street walkers is rising in many North American cities? . . .

Short-Circuited Thinking

Legislation which aims to further criminalize men who pay for sex with adult sex workers and other interventions which aim to 'punish' male clients do not present, as they might at first appear to do, a progressive way forward for feminists and others concerned about improving the rights of women involved in prostitution. In the UK context such policies leave untouched an unsatisfactory legislative framework that undermines the safety and welfare of street sex workers and serves to reinforce the criminal status and hence social stigma associated with sex work. Indeed initiatives such as the KCRP and the associated active policing of street prostitution have the potential to worsen the safety and welfare of women involved in street prostitution, and the most vulnerable women will bear the brunt.

Periodical Bibliography

The following articles have been selected to supplement the diverse views presented in this chapter.

Elaine Audet and Micheline Carrier
"Decriminalize Prostituted Women, Not Prostitution," Sisyphe, November 30, 2004. www.sisyphe.org.

Scott Burris and Daniel Villena
"Adapting to the Reality of HIV," *Human Rights*, Fall 2004.

Steve Chapman
"Fighting a Futile War on Prostitution," *Chicago Tribune*, July 14, 2005.

Susan A. Cohen
"Ominous Convergence: Sex Trafficking, Prostitution, and International Family Planning," *Guttmacher Report on Public Policy*, February 2005.

Concerned Women of America
"Legalizing Prostitution at the U.N.," March 5, 2003. www.cwfa.org.

Leslie Kaufman
"Is the Answer to Child Prostitution Counseling, or Incarceration?" *New York Times*, September 15, 2004.

Michelle Mann
"Dying for Collective Morality," *CBC News*, June 15, 2005.

Richard Poulin
"The Legalization of Prostitution and Its Impact on Trafficking in Women and Children," Sisyphe, February 6, 2005. www.sisyphe.org.

Tracy Quan
"American Laws Against Selling Sex at Odds with 'Sex Sells' Culture," *Knight Ridder/Tribune News Service*, February 26, 2003.

Ivan Wolffers and Nel van Beelen
"Public Health and the Human Rights of Sex Workers," *Lancet*, June 7, 2003.

For Further Discussion

Chapter 1

1. The authors of several viewpoints in this chapter debate whether prostitution and sex trafficking are serious problems. What commonalities among the viewpoints on each side of the debate can you find? Explain, citing from the viewpoints.

2. Jack Shafer and Phelim McAleer both claim that activists exaggerate the number of sex trafficking victims. If Jennifer Goodson and Irena Maryniak were to concede that the number of sex trafficking victims was much lower than reported, what impact if any do you think this concession would have on their claims that the problem of sex trafficking in the United States and Europe is serious? Explain your answer, citing from the viewpoints.

3. If, as Peter McKnight claims, male prostitutes face greater risks than do female prostitutes, are different policies necessary to protect them? Explain, citing similarities and differences between male and female prostitutes cited in the viewpoint.

Chapter 2

1. The editors of the *Economist* claim that society should not view prostitution as a crime; Jillian Blume claims that prostitution empowers some women; Kimberly Klinger believes that for some women prostitution is a choice. What assumption about the sexual exchange between prostitute and customer is necessary to accept these arguments? Have the authors provided evidence to support this assumption? Explain, citing from the viewpoints.

2. Sherry F. Colb contends that while the courts have ruled against imposing criminal penalties for all other consen-

sual sexual practices, society continues to view prostitution as a crime because of the similarity between prostitution and marriage. Based on the evidence Colb provides to support this conclusion, what about marriage would have to change to make it less like prostitution? In your opinion, would these changes be sufficient to decriminalize prostitution? Explain why or why not.

3. Elaine Audet and Melissa Farley see prostitution as a degrading practice that no woman freely chooses. What evidence does each author provide to support her views? Do you find this evidence more or less persuasive than the evidence cited by the *Economist*, Blume, and Klinger? Explain, citing from the viewpoints.

Chapter 3

1. The authors in this chapter, all women, come from several different countries and have different affiliations. How do their backgrounds affect your evaluation of their arguments?

2. The viewpoints of Joy Aghatise Evbuomwan, Kamala Sarup, and Lily Hyde identify different causes for prostitution and sex trafficking. Do these problems suggest a common, root cause of prostitution and sex trafficking? Explain your answer.

3. Which of the policies in Chapter 4 best address each of the factors that the authors claim contribute to prostitution? Do any of the policies that might address one contributing factor conflict with any of the policies that might address other contributing factors? Explain why or why not, citing from the viewpoints.

Chapter 4

1. Mark Liberator argues that prostitution should be legalized and regulated. To support his claim, Liberator com-

pares the government to a business. If the government were a business, he reasons, it would change or eliminate ineffective policies. What is the purpose of a business? What is the purpose of the government? Based on your answers, do you think Liberator's analogy is persuasive? Explain why or why not, citing from the viewpoint.

2. The U.S. Department of State claims that sex-trafficking policies that oppose the legalization of prostitution will reduce sex trafficking. Eartha Melzer argues that such policies hurt prostitutes who have no other way to survive. Which argument do you find more persuasive? Explain.

3. Darla Mueller contends that customers are responsible for most of the violence against prostitutes and that efforts to criminalize customers have effectively protected prostitutes. Rosie Campbell and Merl Storr argue that not all johns are violent and that criminalizing them has increased the danger to prostitutes. Is it necessary to prove whether the customers of prostitutes are or are not violent in order for either claim about the impact of criminalizing customers to be persuasive? Citing the viewpoints, explain why or why not.

Bibliography

Paul R. Abramson, Steven D. Pinkerton, and Mark Huppin	*Sexual Rights in America: The Ninth Amendment and the Pursuit of Happiness.* New York: New York University Press, 2003.
Kevin Bales	*Disposable People: New Slavery in the Global Economy.* Berkeley: University of California Press, 2004.
Joanna Brewis and Stephen Linstead	*Sex Work and Women's Labor Around the World.* Bloomington: Indiana University Press, 2004.
Michel Dorais	*Rent Boys: The World of Male Sex Workers.* Montreal: McGill-Queen's University Press, 2005.
Barbara Ehrenreich and Arlie Russell Hochschild, eds.	*Global Woman: Nannies, Maids, and Sex Workers in the New Economy.* New York: Metropolitan, 2003.
Melissa Farley, ed.	*Prostitution, Trafficking, and Traumatic Stress.* Binghamton, NY: Haworth, 2003.
Kelly Gorkoff and Jane Runner, eds.	*Being Heard: The Experiences of Young Women in Prostitution.* Black Point, Nova Scotia: Fernwood, 2003.

Kamala Kempadoo, ed.	*Trafficking and Prostitution Reconsidered: New Perspectives on Migration, Sex Work, and Human Rights.* Boulder, CO: Paradigm, 2005.
Gilbert King	*Woman, Child for Sale: The New Slave Trade in the 21st Century.* New York: Chamberlain Bros., 2004.
Leonore Kuo	*Prostitution Policy: Revolutionizing Practice Through a Gendered Perspective.* New York: New York University Press, 2002.
David Kyle and Rey Koslowski, eds.	*Global Human Smuggling: Comparative Perspectives.* Baltimore: Johns Hopkins University Press, 2001.
Rachael Lindsay	*Rachael: Woman of the Night.* Cape Town: Kwela, 2003.
Catharine A. MacKinnon	*Women's Lives, Men's Laws.* Cambridge, MA: Belknap, 2005.
Victor Malarek	*The Natashas: Inside the New Global Sex Trade.* New York: Arcade, 2004.
Craig McGill	*Human Traffic: Sex, Slaves, and Immigration.* London: Vision, 2003.

Joyce Outshoorn, ed.	*The Politics of Prostitution: Women's Movements, Democratic States, and the Globalisation of Sex Commerce.* New York: Cambridge University Press, 2004.
Elaine Pearson	*Human Traffic, Human Rights: Redefining Victim Protection.* London: Anti-Slavery International, 2002.
Jody Raphael	*Listening to Olivia: Violence, Poverty, and Prostitution.* Boston: Northeastern University Press, 2004.
Teela Sanders	*Sex Work: A Risky Business.* Portland, OR: Willan, 2005.
Helen J. Self	*Prostitution, Women, and the Misuse of the Law: The Fallen Daughters of Eve.* Portland, OR: Frank Cass, 2003.
Jael Silliman and Anannya Bhattacharjee	*Policing the National Body: Sex, Race, and Criminalization.* Cambridge, MA: South End, 2002.
Siroj Sorajjakool	*Child Prostitution in Thailand: Listening to Rahab.* Binghamton, NY: Haworth, 2003.

David Sterry   *Chicken: Self-Portrait of a Young Man for Rent*. New York: Regan, 2002.

Matt Bernstein Sycamore   *Tricks and Treats: Sex Workers Write About Their Clients*. Binghamton, NY: Haworth, 2000.

Ronald Weitzer, ed.   *Sex for Sale: Prostitution, Pornography, and the Sex Industry*. London: Routledge, 2000.

Organizations to Contact

The Alan Guttmacher Institute
120 Wall St., 21st Fl., New York, NY 10005
(212) 248-1111 • fax: (212) 248-1952
e-mail: info@guttmacher.org
Web site: www.guttmacher.org

The institute works to protect and expand the reproductive choices of all women and men. It strives to ensure that people have access to the information and services they need to exercise their rights and responsibilities concerning sexual activity, reproduction, and family planning. The institute publishes the following bimonthly journals: *Perspectives on Sexual and Reproductive Health*, *International Family Planning Perspectives*, and the *Guttmacher Report on Public Policy*. Selected articles from these publications, including "Ominous Convergence: Sex Trafficking, Prostitution, and International Family Planning" and "Global Concern for Children's Rights: The World Congress Against Sexual Exploitation," are available on its Web site.

American Civil Liberties Union (ACLU)
125 Broad St., 18th Fl., New York, NY 10004-2400
(212) 549-2500
e-mail: aclu@aclu.org
Web site: www.aclu.org

The ACLU champions the human rights set forth in the U.S. Constitution. It works to protect the rights of all Americans and to promote equality for women, minorities, and the poor. The ACLU opposes the U.S.AID requirement that public health organizations and other groups that receive funding under the AIDS Leadership Act must adopt a written policy "explicitly opposing prostitution and sex trafficking." The organization publishes a variety of handbooks, pamphlets, reports, and newsletters, including the quarterly *Civil Liberties* and the monthly *Civil Liberties Alert*. The article "Global AIDS Gag Holds Critical Funding Captive to Politics," is available on its Web site.

Coalition Against Trafficking in Women (CATW)
PO Box 9338, North Amherst, MA 01059
fax: (413) 367-9262
e-mail: info@catwinternational.org
Website: www.catwinternational.org

CATW is a nongovernmental organization that promotes women's human rights. It works internationally to combat sexual exploitation in all its forms, especially prostitution and trafficking in women and children. CATW publishes articles, reports, and speeches on issues related to sex trafficking, including "On the Battlefield of Women's Bodies: An Overview of the Harm of War to Women" and "The Case Against the Legalization of Prostitution," which are available on its Web site.

Concerned Women for America
1015 Fifteenth St. NW, Suite 1100, Washington, DC 20005
(202) 488-7000 • fax: (202) 488-0806
e-mail: mail@cwfa.org
Web site: www.cwfa.org

CWA works to strengthen marriage and the traditional family according to Judeo-Christian moral standards. It opposes abortion, pornography, homosexuality, and the legalization or decriminalization of prostitution. The organization publishes numerous brochures and policy papers as well as *Family Voice*, a monthly newsmagazine. Selected articles opposing the legalization or decriminalization of prostitution such as "Trafficking of Women and Children" are available on its Web site.

Free the Slaves
1012 Fourteenth Street, NW, Suite 600, Washington, DC 20005
(202) 638-1865 • fax: (202) 638-0599
e-mail: info@freetheslaves.net
Web site: www.freetheslaves.net

Free the Slaves dedicates itself to ending slavery worldwide. It partners with grassroots antislavery organizations and concerned businesses to eradicate slavery from product supply chains and to build a consumer movement that chooses slave-free goods. Free the Slaves also encourages governments to draft and enforce effective antislavery and anti-trafficking laws. The organization publishes reports such as International Trafficking in Women to the United States: A Contemporary Manifestation of Slavery and Organized Crime, which is available on its Web site.

Global Rights

1200 Eighteenth Street NW, Suite 602, Washington, DC 20036
(202) 822-4600 • fax: (202) 822-4606
Web site: www.globalrights.org

Global Rights is a human rights advocacy group that partners with local activists worldwide to challenge injustice. The organization opposes U.S. laws that require organizations receiving U.S. global HIV/AIDS and anti-trafficking funds to adopt organization-wide positions opposing prostitution. Global Rights claims that such laws restrict the ability of local activists to prevent the spread of AIDS and to advocate for the health and human rights of women and men in prostitution. It publishes the quarterly magazine *VOICES* and news, reports, and analysis on trafficking. Articles such as "Slavery in Our Midst: The Human Toll of Trafficking" are available on its Web site.

Human Rights Watch

350 Fifth Ave., 34th Fl., New York, NY 10118-3299
(212) 290-4700
e-mail: hrwnyc@hrw.org
Web site: www.hrw.org

Founded in 1978, this nongovernmental organization conducts systematic investigations of human rights abuses in countries around the world, including sex trafficking. It publishes many books and reports on specific countries and issues as well as annual reports, recent selections of which are available on its Web site.

International Justice Mission (IJM)
PO Box 58147, Washington, DC 20037-8147
(703) 465-5495 • fax: (703) 465-5499
e-mail: contact@ijm.org
Web site: www.ijm.org

IJM is a human rights agency that rescues victims of violence, sexual exploitation, slavery, and oppression. Its goals include rescuing victims, bringing accountability under the law to perpetrators, preventing future abuses, and helping victims transition to new lives. IJM publishes articles, reports, and books, including *Terrify No More*, which documents IJM's raids in the Cambodian village of Svay Pak, where its workers rescued thirty-seven underage victims of sex-trafficking, many of them under the age of ten. The book can be purchased on its Web site for a small donation.

International Sex Worker Foundation for Art, Culture, and Education (ISWFACE)
801 Cedros Ave. #7, Panorama City, CA 91402
(818) 892-2029
e-mail: iswface@iswface.org or normaja@webuniverse.net
Web site: www.iswface.org

ISWFACE is an organization run by current and retired sex workers. It serves as an educational resource center for information about and research on prostitution and sex work. Its goal is to foster, perpetuate, and preserve an appreciation of the art and culture created by and about sex workers. Other goals include educating the public about sex workers, their art, and their culture, providing economic alternatives and opportunities for creative, artistic sex workers, and offering accurate, timely information about sex work to health care and law enforcement organizations.

Polaris Project
PO Box 77892, Washington, DC 20013
(202) 547-7990 • fax: (202) 547-6654
e-mail: info@polarisproject.org

Web site: www.polarisproject.org

The Polaris Project is a multicultural grassroots organization combating human trafficking and modern-day slavery. Based in the United States and Japan, it brings together community members, survivors, and professionals to fight trafficking and slavery. The project's goals include empowering trafficking survivors and effecting long-term social change to end trafficking.

Prostitution Research and Education (PRE)
PO Box 16254, San Francisco, CA 94116-0254
e-mail: contact1@prostitutionresearch.com
Web site: www.prostitutionresearch.com

PRE is a nonprofit organization whose goal is to abolish the institution of prostitution. PRE also gives voice to those who are among the world's most disenfranchised groups: prostituted/trafficked women and children. Publications include articles and reports on the legal, social, and health implications of prostitution and sex trafficking, including "Prostitution: Where Racism and Sexism Intersect" and "Prostitution, Violence, and Post-Traumatic Stress Disorder," which are available on its Web site.

Shared Hope International
PO Box 65337, Vancouver, WA 98665
1-866-HER-LIFE
e-mail: savelives@sharedhope.org
Web site: www.sharedhope.org

Shared Hope International is a nonprofit organization that exists to rescue and restore women and children in crisis. It establishes places to which trafficked women and children can escape and receive health care, education, and job training. Shared Hope International works with locally led efforts to rescue trafficked women and children. It also identifies areas of victimization to increase public awareness and builds alliances to eradicate human trafficking. Fact sheets and the article "Tracing the History of Sex Trafficking" are available on its Web site.

Women's Commission on Refugee Women and Children
122 East Forty-second St., 12th Fl.
New York, NY 10168-1289
(212) 551-3088 • fax: (212) 551-3180
e-mail: info@womenscommission.org
Web site: www.womenscommission.org

The commission offers solutions and provides technical assistance to ensure that refugee women, children, and adolescents are protected and have access to education, health services, and livelihood opportunities. It makes recommendations to U.S. and United Nations policy makers and nongovernmental organizations on ways to improve assistance to refugee women and children. Experts conduct field research and technical training in refugee camps and detention centers. On its Web site the commission publishes issues of its semiannual newsletter, *Women's Commission News*, reports, and articles, including "The Struggle Between Migration Control and Victim Protection: The UK Approach to Human Trafficking."

World Vision International
800 West Chestnut Ave., Monrovia, CA 91016
(626) 303-8811
e-mail: newsvision@wvi.org
Web site: www.wvi.org

Established in 1950, World Vision International is a Christian relief and development organization that works for the well-being of all people, especially children. Through emergency relief, education, health care, economic development, and promotion of justice, World Vision's goal is to help communities help themselves. It publishes the quarterly *Global Future* and many reports and articles, many of which are available on its Web site, including "Children's Work, Adult's Play: Child Sex Tourism—The Problem in Cambodia."

Index